The Secondary School Assemblies Resource Book

First published in Great Britain in 2007
Society for Promoting Christian Knowledge
36 Causton Street
London SW1P 4ST

The author and publisher have made every effort to ensure
that the external website and email addresses included in
this book are correct and up to date at the time of going to
press. The author and publisher are not responsible for the
content, quality or continuing accessibility of the sites.

British Library Cataloguing-in-Publication Data

A catalogue record for this book
is available from the British Library

ISBN 978-0-281-05892-1

Typeset by PDQ Typesetting Ltd, Newcastle-under-Lyme
Printed in Great Britain by Ashford Colour Press

Contents

Introduction

If you're reading this book, the chances are you are about to stand in front of a group of teenagers and give an assembly – and, more than likely, within the next ten minutes!

If you are pressed for time, may I wish you every success in what is often an exceedingly demanding but ultimately very rewarding part of teaching, but suggest you get a move on, find an assembly and read the rest of this later when you're less stressed! However, if you aren't standing outside the assembly hall desperately flicking through to find something interesting to perform, please read on.

I use the word 'perform', because that's exactly what you are doing when you give assemblies. The young people you are trying to engage with are extremely sophisticated and are accustomed to their world being presented to them in a highly polished and professional manner. These information consumers are very selective about which messages they choose to heed and anything that is considered outdated or irrelevant will quickly be consigned to their mental equivalent of the junk mail file in your email folder.

You are competing against the messages sent out from TV, advertising, the internet and games systems. These are multimillion pound affairs devised by marketing firms whose subtlety and persuasiveness are second to none. All you have to offer is your personality, your sincerity and (hopefully) your genuine concern for the students in your care. Having said that, make no mistake: a well thought out assembly that actively engages with the audience and attempts to present ultimate truths in a persuasive and sympathetic manner can be as affective and effective as any TV advert.

It should be thought provoking, actively engaging and, above all, enjoyable. Nobody likes being preached at, and worse still nagged. If an assembly merely becomes an opportunity to moan and berate then any shred of educational or spiritual development is completely lost.

Your assembly should always aim to provide opportunities for students to consider spiritual and moral issues; explore their own beliefs and those of others; experience prayer (whether they choose to engage with it personally or not); appreciate the importance of religious beliefs to those who hold them; think about the needs of others; develop a sense of community spirit; promote a common ethos and shared ideals and, most of all, appreciate and develop positive values. This all sounds a tall order, but over the course of the year sensitive delivery of good quality material will certainly go some way towards making this a positive and worthwhile time in the school day and have genuine educational value.

Have no doubt that giving an assembly is as much about teaching and learning as any lesson you give in your subject area and should be planned in exactly the same way. It should have a clear beginning, middle and end, and should actively engage with the audience, differentiate for all learning types and have a clear aim and message that will remain after the assembly is finished and be talked about days after. There is nothing more satisfying than students harking back to one of your assemblies long after you've given it: 'Remember when you did that funny assembly, Sir?' Priceless!

The assemblies in this book are taken from the Assemblies website <www.assemblies.org.uk> and have been devised by practising teachers who are engaged in their delivery every week. They are tried and tested and in most cases represent key elements of good practice in assembly delivery. Some require more preparation than others, but most are designed to be picked up and performed with very little fuss or bother. All of them are intended to be interesting, appealing and thought provoking.

The assemblies selected for this collection are organized under five headings: 'Through the Year', which contains assemblies connected to Christian seasons and key times of the school year; 'How to Live', containing words of wisdom and advice on daily life and behaviour; 'Awe and Wonder', in which assemblies look at the ultimate issues of life; 'Christian Ideas', mainly about the Bible; and 'Inspiring People', concerned with Christians whose lives are an example to others. There is also a final section of 'Assemblets'.

What are assemblets?

Story-tellers from Aesop to Roald Dahl knew the advantages of brief tales to capture their audience's attention and provide clear moral advice or warnings.

Busy assembly-givers sometimes need a short, snappy story with a clear simple moral – especially when they are pushed for time but still want to give their audience an effective message. That's why we have created 'assemblets'.

Assemblets are short moral tales, sometimes funny, sometimes thought-provoking, that should disarm the listener and make even the briefest assembly opportunity worthwhile. They can easily be committed to memory and so can give the assembly-giver that sense of spontaneity that is often lacking.

Assemblets are extremely versatile and can also be used in class assemblies or as part of a larger act of worship where smaller readings are appropriate.

Often students have become immune to long drawn-out assemblies, so try an assemblet to catch their attention. Above all, they should at least keep your students keen to hear more.

Go for it

Giving an assembly takes a certain amount of courage and self-confidence. It's like doing a huge lesson and usually involves being observed by numerous colleagues and senior managers. For all that, don't be afraid to have fun with it. Make it a joyous occasion – it's worth the effort. Your audience will appreciate that you have done something interesting and fresh, and your colleagues will either admire you for your expertise or just be relieved that they haven't had to take assembly.

Good assemblies are at the heart of what good schools should be about. What are you waiting for?

STUART KERNER
Secondary Schools Assemblies Editor
www.assemblies.org.uk

P.S. If you think you have any assemblies as good as, or better than, those that follow, please don't hesitate to submit them to us at <assemblies@spck.org.uk>.

A note about the songs

Most of the songs recommended for assemblies in this book come from either *The Complete Come and Praise* (BBC Educational Publishing, 1988) or *Complete Mission Praise* (expanded edition, Collins, 2005). The songs are numbered as found in these publications.

Through the Year

A NEW START

By *Stuart Kerner*

Suitable for Key Stage Three

Aim

To think about the start of a new school year and the possibilities that lie ahead.

Preparation and materials

- A calculator would be very useful for the opening stunt.
- Bible reading: the parable of the talents (Matthew 25.14–29).
- Music: 'Things can only get better' by D:Ream.

Assembly

1. Begin the assembly by welcoming the students back after the holiday and tell them you spent your vacation learning how to read minds, which you will now prove.
2. Select two volunteers, and ask them to stand at the front. Give each a calculator and run through the following stages, during which you should pretend to be mystically reading their minds.
3. Ask each volunteer to pick a number from 1 to 10.
   Subtract 5.
   Multiply by 3.
   Square it/multiply it by itself.
   Add the digits of the resulting number until you get a single digit (for example, 169 = 1 + 6 + 9 = 16 = 1 + 6 = 7).
   Now, if the number is greater than 5 subtract 4, otherwise add 5.
   Multiply by 2.
   Subtract 6.
   If your answer is 1 pick A, if 2 pick B, if 3 pick C, and so on.

4. Give your volunteers a piece of paper and ask them to write down a country that starts with the letter they picked.
5. Now write down the name of a mammal that starts with the second letter from the name of the country they picked.
6. Write down the colour of that mammal.
7. Tell your hapless victims, 'You have a grey elephant from Denmark', and ask them to show the audience. Thank them, and send them back to the audience with a round of applause.
8. Now tell your audience that although that was an amazing feat, your powers are limited. You can't, for instance, see into the future. Each of us creates our own future based on the hard work and commitment we put into things. Consequently, you don't know what will happen during this school year.
9. A new school year brings with it new opportunities and new challenges. Perhaps we didn't do as well as we had hoped last year. Now we can put our disappointing performance behind us. Maybe there are things we want to try to do differently.
10. We may make new friends, and possibly grow apart from old ones. We will study new subjects, have new teachers and the amount of homework we are expected to do will almost certainly increase!
11. In among all of these new experiences, which seem just to come upon us, it is important to remember that we are the ones who decide how well or how badly we will do in life. Success is not something that just happens, we must work at it. Sir Francis Bacon, an English philosopher and statesman said: 'A wise man will make more opportunities than he finds.'
12. You have to make up your mind, as this year begins, whether or not you are going to be a success. You have also to decide how you are going to do all you have to do. Some people don't try very hard because they are afraid of failure, but we should remember the fact that failure is success if we learn from it.
13. Finish by telling the students to imagine that you can tell the future. What would they want you to tell them about their

lives in a year's time? Remind them that they have the power to make it come true.

 Time for reflection

Close your eyes.
In your mind's eye form a picture of yourself in a year's time.
Make the picture big, bold and bright.
Do you look happy or sad?
Do you look successful or downhearted?
Have you achieved all you hoped for?
Now consider how you're going to make this image a reality.
Think about what this new year might be like for you.
Are you looking forward to it?
Are there things you're nervous about?
Are there things you'd like to do better than last year?
What new chance would you like this year?
How would you like to be different?
Say to yourself, 'Only I can make this happen.'

Heavenly Father,
Thank you for the chance to begin again.
Help us to take fully the new opportunities that present themselves.
May we concentrate on achieving our best,
and give us the will to aim for higher standards in all we do.
Amen.

 Song

'Lord of all hopefulness' (*Come and Praise*, 52)

HARVEST

By Helen Lycitt

Suitable for Key Stage Three

Aim

To remember those in need around the world and encourage students to change their attitudes towards them.

Preparation and materials

- Seven A4 sheets with the letters H A R V E S T printed or written on them, one letter on each sheet.
- Different foods from around the world.
- Information on fair trade:
  www.christian-aid.org.uk/campaign/index.htm
  www.traidcraft.co.uk/
  www.unicef.org/
  www.tearfund.org/
  www.cafod.org.uk/
- Music: 'Harvest for the World' by The Christians

Assembly

1. Introduce the assembly by telling your audience that today you want to consider what harvest is really all about.
2. You will need seven volunteers. Provide each volunteer with one of the A4 sheets. Get them to stand so that they spell the word HARVEST.
3. Ask the volunteers to arrange themselves so that the letters spell EARTH. (The two left over should be encouraged to stand aside.)
4. Comment that at this time of year we remember and celebrate all the wonderful resources that the earth provides. Show some of the examples of food that you have and briefly

explain how hard it can be for people in many parts of the world to get a fair price for producing things we take for granted.

5. Ask the volunteers to move so that their letters spell the word STARVE.

6. Ask students how often they go home and say things like, 'I'm starving!', when all they really mean is, 'I'm very hungry.' Each day, all around the world people really are starving, many do not know where their next meal is coming from, and many more will die from malnutrition.

7. Suggest that we should stop taking our food for granted and stop wasting so much.

8. Prompt your volunteers to spell the word SHARE.

9. Remind students how lucky we are to have food in abundance. Observe that, as Gandhi said, there is enough for everyone's need, but not enough for everyone's greed.

10. Suggest that they might like to give up eating something (for example, a favourite chocolate bar) for two weeks and donate the money to a charity such as Christian Aid, Tearfund or Cafod.

11. If we share what we have in abundance, we can begin to create a harvest for the world.

12. Ask your volunteers to spell out HEART.

13. Observe that giving money at this time of year is an important way of helping the most needy in the world, but that this is only superficial. What we really need is to make a change of heart.

14. We must consider our lifestyle and find a way to live more simply so that those people suffering and starving might simply live.

Other words you could incorporate into this assembly include:
HAVES (we are the 'haves', we must consider the 'have nots');
EARS (you could encourage them to use these to listen to your message);
HASTE (encourage them to act now on global poverty);
VAST (to exemplify the scale of the problem);
REST (perhaps an alternative way to end, suggest you need one!).

Time for reflection

This prayer can be said either with or without the A4 letters.

> Lord,
> HARVEST time is here again.
> We HAVE brought THE flowers, fruit and vegetables
> that we HAVE grown in THE summer HEAT.
> We STARE AT THE HARVEST of EARTH and SEA.
> We RAVE over THE lovely flowers arranged in A VASE.
> Thank you, Lord God, for HARVEST.
>
> We throw good food away as TRASH for RATS to EAT
> AT an alarming RATE.
> We HAVE so much; while millions STARVE.
> SAVE us from greed and selfishness.
> Help us, Lord, to SHARE THE good things you HAVE
>   given,
> that everyone may HAVE enough to EAT,
> STAVE off THE pangs of hunger and AVERT starvation.
> Take away all HATE from our HEARTS
> and fill THE EARTH with your love
> from EAST to west and back again.
> HEAR our prayer, Lord of the HARVEST.
> **Amen.**

 Song

'For the fruits of his creation' (*Mission Praise*, 153)

ST ANDREW'S DAY

By *Stuart Kerner*

Suitable for Whole School

Aim

To reflect on the importance of trusting our lives to God.

Preparation and materials

- Four volunteers, two apples and two peelers.

Assembly

1. Ask the students if anyone can name the patron saints of England, Scotland, Wales and Ireland (St George, St Andrew, St David and St Patrick).

2. Say that 30 November is St Andrew's Day. St Andrew, like his brother Peter, was originally a fisherman. He became one of the first disciples of Jesus, and, according to tradition, went on to spread the gospel in Syria, Turkey, Russia and Greece. Legend has it that he was eventually crucified on an X-shaped cross.

3. On St Andrew's Day people of Scottish origins all over the world celebrate their heritage. Although St Andrew's Day celebrations used to be very popular in Scotland itself, this is no longer the case. In a recent survey, one in four Scottish people didn't even know the date of St Andrew's Day!

4. In some places, St Andrew's Day was traditionally a day for young girls to try to find out about their future husbands. By way of demonstration, ask for two volunteers and tell them to remove their left shoes. This will, no doubt, create some amusement. Say that one Scottish legend has it that on St Andrew's Day a girl wishing to marry should throw a shoe over her shoulder towards a doorway. If the toe of the shoe

pointed in the direction of the exit, then she would marry and leave her parents' house within a year.

5. Instruct your (shoeless) volunteers to face away from a door and throw their shoes towards it. Inform them of the result, and make light of it – perhaps they had better let their parents know that they could soon rent out their room! Allow them to retrieve their footwear and return to their seats with a round of applause.

6. Ask for two more volunteers and give them each an apple and a peeler. Tell them to try to peel their apple without breaking the peel (the result is likely to be less than perfect, but that need not spoil the effect). Say that another Scottish legend has it that if on St Andrew's Day a person peels a whole apple without breaking the peel and throws the long spiral of peel over their shoulder, they can deduce the first letter of their future husband's or wife's name from the shape of the peel on the floor.

7. Show the audience how well (or not) your volunteers have done their peeling before instructing them both to fling the peel over their shoulder. Again, let everyone know the outcome, before releasing your volunteers with a round of applause.

8. Comment that of course these are just superstitions dreamed up to satisfy our curiosity about future events in our lives. In fact, none of us knows what God has in store for us – just as the humble fisherman Andrew had no idea how important his life would be. We must wait and see. What we do know is that God has a plan for us, just as he had for Andrew.

9. You may wish to add that the Bible tells us not to worry about our future. Jesus said, 'Do not worry about tomorrow: tomorrow will take care of itself. Each day has enough trouble of its own' (Matthew 6.34).

 Time for reflection

These words were written by St Columba, Scotland's original patron saint, who was born in the sixth century:

Be at peace, and love each other.
Follow the example of good people

and God will comfort and help you,
now and in the future.

 Song

'Fear not, rejoice and be glad' (*Mission Praise*, 144)

PART OF THE DISEASE OR PART OF THE CURE? AN ASSEMBLY ON WAR FOR REMEMBRANCE DAY

By Guy Donegan-Cross

Suitable for Whole School

 Aim

To reflect on the sacrifice made in wars and the sacrifice of Christ.

 Preparation and materials

None required.

 Assembly

1. Today is Remembrance Day, a good opportunity to remember all who have died in war. Refer to a current military conflict. Ask the children what they think about it. Ask: 'In a world full of war, are you part of the disease or the cure?'

2. War has always been part of the human condition. A group of academics and historians has compiled this startling information:

   - Since 3600 BC, the world has known only 292 years of peace!
   - During this period, there have been 14,351 wars large and small, in which 3.64 billion people have been killed.
   - The value of the property destroyed is equal to a golden belt around the world 97.2 miles wide and 10 metres thick.
   - Since 650 BC, there have also been 1,656 arms races, only 16 of which have not ended in war.

3. Two stories about war challenge me:

A man called Tony Campolo remembers being interviewed by the Draft Board for military service back in the 1950s. Finding out that he was a Christian, an Air Force officer asked Tony if he were a 'conscientious objector'. Tony had no idea what that meant, so the officer asked him, 'If you were in a bomber flying over an enemy city, and you knew there were civilians down there, would you still go ahead and drop the bombs?'

'I'm not sure,' Tony replied. 'I guess I'd have to pray, and ask Jesus what he'd do.'

'That's ridiculous!' exclaimed the Air Force officer, mentally dismissing Tony as an idiot and marking him unsuitable. 'Everyone knows Jesus wouldn't drop bombs.'

Everyone needs a way to live. For people who are Christians the main thing we ask ourselves is what would Jesus do. What about you? Where do you get your guidance from? How do you know if you are part of the disease or the cure?

4. My second story is about sacrifice:

A marine recruit was assigned to take basic training at Paris Island – an army barracks. He was one of those young men who seemed to be a bit out of step with the norm, and he quickly became the object of ridicule by those who enjoy picking on offbeat people.

In the barracks to which this young marine was assigned, there was an extremely high level of meanness. The other young men did everything they could to turn the new recruit into a joke and to humiliate him.

One day someone came up with the bright idea that they could scare the daylights out of this young marine by dropping a disarmed hand grenade on to the floor and pretending it was about to go off. Everyone else knew about this and they were all ready to get a big laugh.

The hand grenade was thrown into the middle of the room and the warning was yelled: 'It's a live grenade! It's a live grenade! It's about to explode!'

They fully expected that the young man would get hysterical and perhaps jump out of a window. Instead, he fell on the grenade, hugged it to his stomach, and yelled to the other men in the barracks, 'Run for your lives! Run for your lives! You'll be killed if you don't!'

The other marines froze in shame. They realized that the one they had scorned was the one ready to lay down his life for them.

5. When it comes to Remembrance Day, I think of two people who laid down their lives for me: Jesus, who said on the cross, 'Father, forgive them'; and the unknown soldier, who represents all those with the courage to give up their lives. For both of them I want to take war seriously – to be part of the cure, and not part of the disease.

 ## Time for reflection

God of love,
Prince of Peace,
may I be part of the cure,
part of the solution
in this suffering world.
Amen.

 ## Song

'Peace, perfect peace' (*Come and Praise*, 53)

WAITING – ADVENT

By Stuart Kerner

Suitable for Whole School

 Aim

To introduce Advent as a time of waiting and preparation.

 Preparation and materials

None required.

 Assembly

1. Begin by standing in front of your audience. Look as though you are about to say something, then abruptly stop, look flustered and tell them to hang on. Leave the assembly hall for a moment (any longer may make it difficult to regain their attention), then return to the front. Again, look as though you are about to start, stop, tell them to hang on again, pause, look around and then finally say: Don't you hate being kept waiting?

2. For Christians this is the season of Advent – the beginning of the Christian year. It is a time for waiting patiently. It is a reminder to get ready for the 'advent' or coming of Jesus Christ. It isn't just a reminder to start buying cards and presents, or make the Christmas cake, or even think about Jesus' first coming at Christmas. Advent reminds us that Jesus is coming again. The first Christians expected Jesus to come back at any time. Centuries have passed but Jesus' promise to return still stands firm.

3. These days we have become very bad at waiting. Every year the Christmas season seems to start earlier and earlier. Christmas gift catalogues are sent out in August. We find decorations and seasonal items in the shops long before

Bonfire Night. Adverts on the TV begin showing Father Christmas from the middle of October.

4. 'Wait!' we say. 'It's not time yet!' Rushing the season only spoils it. But modern life makes us very impatient. We have email. We have instant text messages on our mobiles. We have fast food. We can't drive 50 miles an hour when we can go 70. We want answers to our questions and our prayers and we want them right now!

5. And in the midst of all that rush and unnecessary hurry we must learn to be patient. The time is almost here. God's promise is sure. He will come again soon. Meanwhile, let things happen in their season. Let the rain and snow come in their time. Let the days grow shorter. Let the nights get colder. It's all right. God has promised he will return, and his promises are sure.

6. After all, we know what to expect, and it will certainly be worth the wait!

Time for reflection

Read these verses from James 5.7–8:

Be patient, therefore, beloved, until the coming of the Lord. The farmer waits for the precious crop from the earth, being patient with it until it receives the early and the late rains. You also must be patient. Strengthen your hearts, for the coming of the Lord is near.

Lord,
As we make our lists,
and put up our decorations,
as we write our Christmas cards,
and buy our presents,
help us to stand back and remember
that it isn't really Christmas yet.
Help us to take time to wait,
to be patient,
to sense the tranquillity of expectation,
and to appreciate fully the magnitude of your imminent
   coming.
Amen.

Song

'O what a gift!' (*Mission Praise*, 526)

AND THE WORD WAS MADE FLESH

By Helen Lycitt

Suitable for Whole School

 Aim

To reflect on the Word of God being made flesh at Christmas.

 Preparation and materials

- An OHP transparency showing the three sayings (see point 1).

 Assembly

1. Using the OHP transparency, show your audience these three sayings: 'Fine words butter no parsnips', 'All mouth and no trousers' and 'Hard words break no bones'.
2. Ask for ideas to explain what these sayings mean. Hopefully someone will correctly answer with something like, 'They all show contempt for people who talk a lot but do little.'
3. Continue by asking the students, whether they would rather be someone who is known for their words or someone known for their actions. Most of us would probably say the latter.
4. Point out that it is strange, then, that at Christmas we are told that God's Word became something amazing – Christ, who would be our saviour. As it says at the beginning of John's Gospel in the New Testament: 'In the beginning was the Word ... and the Word was God.'

    So to compare God, born in the form of man, to a word, and to describe him, as John later does, as 'the Word made flesh' is, so to speak, to get him off to a bad start in people's minds.
5. Of course, getting off to a bad start applies to a good many things that people can't be bothered, or are unable, to look at

closely. Try to read a book or a newspaper from a distance, or the destination of a bus when it's too far away to see properly, and you'll learn nothing. Look at them more closely and they may become much more interesting. The bus may even be going where you want it to!

6. The same is also true of the spoken word. To hear voices speaking when they're some distance away, or hearing them, but not listening to what is being said, will result in your not understanding anything. Get closer, listen carefully, and you may well find they're about something really important and interesting.

7. So we can begin to see that words are far more powerful than we first thought.

8. Of course, many people turn a deaf ear to the word of God. Then there have always been others who hear but do not listen. There's not very much we can do about that and from the very earliest times Christians, following Jesus' advice, left those who would not hear, shook the dust off their feet, and went to proclaim the word to someone else.

9. On the first Christmas Day only a tiny handful of people heard the message of the angels or the baby crying in the manger. Today the word of God is heard and followed all over the world. Perhaps words can be as powerful as actions after all.

 Time for reflection

Lord,
Help us to realize that although our own words are limited,
   yours are not.
Help us to comprehend that although our existence is sinful,
   yours is not.
Help us to appreciate that although our love is finite,
   yours is not;
through Jesus Christ, the Word made flesh.
Amen.

 Song

'How sweet the name of Jesus sounds' (*Mission Praise*, 251)

WOT NO SANTA?

By Helen Hinxman

Suitable for Key Stage Three

Aim

To provide something silly for Christmas – with a serious point about the meaning of the festival.

Preparation and materials

- You might like to wear a white laboratory coat as you present your research evidence, and perhaps prepare a folder with 'SANTA RESEARCH PROJECT' in big letters, or a flipchart with suitable diagrams.
- Suggested music: 'Santa Claus is coming to town' by J. Fred Coots and Haven Gillespie.

Assembly

1. Ask the students how many of them believed in Father Christmas when they were younger. You should get a large show of hands.
2. Now ask them to raise their hands if they still believe he exists and delivers their presents each year. (Hopefully, a smaller number.)
3. Explain that, as with many things, the existence of Santa Claus is something of a mystery, but fortunately you have conducted in-depth scientific research into the matter and can conclusively report that he does not, in fact, exist.
4. Present the following information, using your best, rapid-fire, stereotypical scientist's voice:

   - We know of no species of reindeer that can fly. But it is estimated that there are 300,000 species of living organisms yet to be classified, and while most of these are insects and germs, this does not completely rule out flying reindeer, which only Santa has ever seen.

- There are 2 billion children (persons under 18) in the world. If you take away the children from families of non-Christian faiths, that reduces Santa's workload to 15 per cent of the total – 378 million.
- At an average rate of 3.5 children per household, that's 91.8 million homes. One assumes there's at least one good child in each.
- Santa has 31 hours of Christmas to work with, thanks to the different time zones and the rotation of the earth, assuming he travels east to west (which seems logical). This works out to 822.6 visits per second.
- This is to say that for each Christian household with good children, Santa has one-thousandth of a second to do the following: park, hop out of the sleigh, jump down the chimney, fill the stockings, distribute the remaining presents under the tree, eat whatever snacks have been left, climb back up the chimney, get back into the sleigh and move on to the next house.
- Assuming that each of these 91.8 million stops are evenly distributed around the earth (which, of course, we know to be false but for the purposes of our calculations we will accept), we are talking about 0.78 miles between each household, a total trip of 75½ million miles, not counting toilet stops (which most of us must do at least once every 31 hours – especially after drinking all those glasses of milk and sherry!). This means that Santa's sleigh is moving at 650 miles per second, 3,000 times the speed of sound.
- The weight of the sleigh's cargo adds another interesting element. Assuming that each child gets nothing more than a medium-sized Lego set (weighing 2 pounds), the sleigh is carrying 321,300 tons, not counting Santa, who is invariably described as overweight.
- On land, conventional reindeer can pull no more than 300 pounds. Even granting that 'flying reindeer' could pull ten times the normal amount, we cannot do the job with eight, or even nine. We need 214,200 reindeer. This increases the

overall weight – not counting the sleigh itself – to 353,430 tons.

- 353,000 tons travelling at 650 miles per second creates enormous air resistance. This will heat the reindeer up rather like a spacecraft re-entering the earth's atmosphere.
- The lead pair of reindeer will absorb 14.3 quintillion joules of energy per second – each. In short, they will burst into flame almost instantaneously, exposing the reindeer behind them, and create deafening sonic booms. The entire reindeer team will be vaporized within 4.26 thousandths of a second.
- Santa, meanwhile, will be subjected to forces 17,500.09 times greater than gravity. This means that an 18-stone Santa (which seems ludicrously slim) would be pinned to the back of his sleigh by 4,315,015 pounds of force.
- In conclusion – if Santa ever did deliver presents on Christmas Eve, he only did it the once, before disappearing in a cloud of smoke!

5. Of course, without Santa Claus to bring us presents we need to ensure that we give each other something at this special time of the year. Let us begin by loving one another, caring for all and making the spirit of Christmas last all year round.

 ## Time for reflection

Why Jesus is better than Santa Claus!

Santa lives at the North Pole: Jesus is everywhere.

Santa rides in a sleigh: Jesus rides on the wind and walks on the water.

Santa comes but once a year: Jesus is an ever-present help.

Santa fills your stockings with goodies: Jesus supplies all your needs.

Santa comes down your chimney uninvited: Jesus stands at your door and knocks, and then enters your heart when invited.

You have to wait in line to see Santa: Jesus is as close as the mention of his name.

Santa lets you sit on his lap: Jesus lets you rest in his arms.

Santa doesn't know your name, all he can say is, 'Hi, little boy or girl, what's your name?': Jesus knew our name before we were born. Not only does he know our name, he knows our address, too. He knows our history and future and he even knows how many hairs are on our heads.

Santa has a belly like a bowlful of jelly: Jesus has a heart full of love.

All Santa can offer is, 'Ho, ho, ho': Jesus offers health, help and hope.

Santa says, 'You better not cry': Jesus says, 'Cast all your cares on me for I care for you.'

Santa's little helpers make toys: Jesus makes new life, mends wounded hearts, repairs broken homes and builds mansions.

Santa may make you chuckle, but: Jesus gives you joy that is your strength.

While Santa puts gifts under your tree Jesus became our gift and died on a tree – the cross.

We need to put Christ back in CHRISTmas.

Jesus is still the reason for the season!

 Song

'Christmas, Christmas' (*Come and Praise*, 122)

EPIPHANY

By Stuart Kerner

Suitable for Whole School

Aim

To understand the purpose of the coming of Jesus.

Preparation and materials

- Bible reading: Luke 2.25–32.

Assembly

1. Begin by asking if anyone made a New Year's resolution last week. Contributions might include diets, walking to school, or giving money to charity.

2. A New Year's resolution is a promise that you will change some aspect of your life. Generally New Year resolutions are private matters for the well-being of the people making them. The habits of chocoholics or fast food freaks usually only affect the lives of others if their diet eventually brings poor health.

   Some resolutions, however, are promises made to other people. Some people promise to spend more time with their families or to do more for other people. Others promise their bosses that they will work harder at their jobs. Even children get involved by promising their parents and teachers that they will spend more time on their homework and less time on their computer games!

3. When we fail to keep the resolutions that affect those around us, we're breaking promises we've made to them. Promises are important, but in our society we have become conditioned to the fact that promises are sometimes not kept. So we take them and make them lightly. When we

23

watch television, we are constantly bombarded with advertisements that promise that a particular product will make our lives better. Our teeth will be whiter, our clothes cleaner, our bodies healthier. At New Year, we make promises that we will probably fail to keep.

4. Human beings have difficulty keeping promises, but there is one who is consistent. God keeps his promises. He did so throughout the history of Israel, always fulfilling his word. He finally fulfilled his promises to Israel in the birth of Jesus.

   Many of God's promises were personal, given to men and women of faith who waited patiently for God's word to be proved true. When Joseph and Mary took Jesus to the temple to be circumcised eight days after he was born, for instance, two people saw the fulfilment of God's promises made to them personally. One of these people was Simeon.

5. Read Luke 2.25–32.

6. The word 'Epiphany' means 'the appearance of a divine being'. At Epiphany the Church recognizes that through the wise men God revealed the nature of Jesus to the world. But it was not only to these travellers that the newborn Jesus was revealed.

7. Apart from Simeon, the other person to be blessed when the baby Jesus was taken to the temple was a prophetess named Anna. She never left the temple, but worshipped there night and day, fasting and praying. She came up to Mary and Joseph, praising God and speaking about the child.

   Simeon and Anna were both blessed with a moment in the presence of their Saviour and the knowledge of the true identity of the child they held. God had promised this would be, and ensured that his promises were fulfilled.

8. In today's society when promises are taken lightly, when resolutions are easily set aside, we have one in whom we can have absolute trust. Though our family and friends may break their promises, God will never do so. Rest assured that whatever God has planned for your life will come to be.

Time for reflection

God became like us, so that we might become like him.

> Lord of life, you who keep your promises,
> through your incarnation inspire us to do the same.
> As you appeared to Anna and Simeon, and the wise men,
> show yourself in our lives,
> that we may come to know you
> and trust in your great vision for humanity.
> **Amen.**

 Song

'O Jesus, I have promised' (*Mission Praise, 501*)

ST VALENTINE'S DAY

By *Stuart Kerner*

Suitable for Whole School

 Aim

To consider what love really means.

 Preparation and materials

- Prepare a large photocopy, OHP transparency or PowerPoint slide of the statue of Eros: some good places to find a picture on the internet include:
  www.coe.uncc.edu/~sherlock/Personal/Summer2000/
  523517/Medium12.jpg
  www.mjausson.com/2002/img/25Jun02_London/11eros_
  sky.jpg
- Some Valentine's Day cards with pictures of Eros/Cupid.

 Assembly

1. Find out from the students how many of them either sent or received a Valentine card. Tell them that nobody can say for sure who St Valentine was; and there is nothing to connect him to the custom of sending anonymous cards to our sweethearts – although many different theories exist. Comment that it is funny how facts and myths get confused.
2. Now ask if anyone has ever been to Piccadilly Circus in London. At the very least, they will probably have 'bought' Piccadilly while playing Monopoly. Say that in the centre of Piccadilly Circus there is a statue of a winged man wearing only a loincloth. He's standing on one leg above a bronze fountain and is firing a bow and arrow. This figure, made of aluminium, is usually known as 'Eros': show the picture of the statue.

3. Explain that Eros was the Greek god of love. He would shoot his arrows into the hearts of gods or mortals to arouse their desires. His arrows came in two types: golden with dove feathers, which aroused love, or leaden arrows with owl feathers, which caused lack of interest. Eros would make as much mischief as he possibly could by wounding the hearts of all. The Romans borrowed Eros from the Greeks, and named him Cupid. Pictures of Eros or Cupid often appear on Valentine cards – as the students may have seen on those they sent or received. If you have some cards, show them now to illustrate your point.

4. In reality, the truth is that the statue in Piccadilly is not of a pagan god at all. It is actually called The Shaftesbury Monument and represents the angel of Christian charity. It was put up in 1892 as a tribute to a man called Anthony Ashley Cooper, the seventh Earl of Shaftesbury. One of the streets leading from Piccadilly Circus is also named after the Earl of Shaftesbury. Today Shaftesbury Avenue is home to many of London's top theatres.

5. Say to the children:
You may have heard of Lord Shaftesbury in history. As a boy he was uncared for and mistreated. His father bullied him. Bringing him to start at boarding school, his father punched his son at the door and advised the tutor to do the same. Anthony carried the mental scars of this abuse with him all his life. However, good eventually came out of this cruelty to the sensitive boy as he was always able to sympathize with the sufferings of others.

In 1826 Shaftesbury became a Member of Parliament. As a Christian, he was shocked to learn of the horrors of life for the working classes in England. He toured the slums, workhouses and asylums to see for himself what conditions were like before presenting his evidence to his fellow MPs for action to be taken.

A list of all the social causes Shaftesbury championed would fill an entire page.

- He founded schools long before the government took responsibility for education.

- He pressed for improved sewage systems to prevent diseases like cholera.
- He campaigned to bring an end to women and children being forced to haul coal for long hours in the darkness of the mines.
- Young boys were freed from work as chimney sweeps thanks to his determination.
- He fought against child prostitution.
- He did all he could to see that starving children were properly fed.
- He supported better housing for the poor.

6. All of this was guided by one simple idea. Shaftesbury was fierce in his conviction that Jesus must be at the centre of people's lives, and that through love we can all achieve our true potential. Because of this, Shaftesbury was a popular, well-loved figure. When he preached people listened with respect. At his funeral, thousands stood without hats in the pouring rain to show their love for the man who had loved them.

7. In the New Testament St Paul tells us what Christian love ought to be:

> Love is patient and kind. It does not envy, it does not boast, it is not proud. It is not rude, it is not selfish, it is not easily angered, and it forgets mistakes. Love does not take pleasure in evil but celebrates with the truth. It always protects, always trusts, always hopes, and it never gives up.
>
> *1 Corinthians 13.4–7*

 Time for reflection

Stop and think.
How do I show love towards other people?
What can I do for other people today?

Dear God,
Make us patient and kind,

and help us to resist envy.
Prevent us from boasting,
and protect us from pride.
Forgive us when we are rude or selfish,
and stop us if our temper gets the better of us.
Help us to avoid evil,
and encourage us to be truthful.
That we may bring true love into our own lives,
and share it with those we meet each day.
Amen.

 Song

'Love divine, all loves excelling' (*Mission Praise*, 449)

WHAT IS LENT?

By Sophie Jelley

Suitable for Key Stage Three

 Aim

To explain the idea of Lent as a period of self-examination for Christians.

 Preparation and materials

- A few chairs pushed together to make a bed.
- A white coat borrowed from the Science Department.

 Assembly

1. Ask what day comes after Pancake Day or Shrove Tuesday: Ash Wednesday. Say that Ash Wednesday is the first day of Lent, which is the time in the year when Christians remember the 40 days when God's Son, Jesus, went off into the wilderness to spend time alone with his Father God. The date of Ash Wednesday is worked out by counting back 40 weekdays from Easter Saturday.

2. Lent is one of the two seasons in the year (the other one is Advent – before Christmas) when Christians think especially about how their lives match up to the way God wants them to live. It is a bit like having a spiritual medical.

3. Explain that you have set up a makeshift doctor's surgery in school today (put on your white coat). Ask for a volunteer to be the patient (quietly assure your volunteer that you will not embarrass them in any way and they will not be required to remove any item of clothing).

4. Work from the top down, and as you examine each part of the body, speak to the patient first and then to the audience. Ask the patient an appropriate question: 'Any pain? Any

shortness of breath?', etc. Declare that part of the body to be healthy, then say to your audience:

- Head – we may be well in the head but how are our thoughts? The Bible says that we should think about whatever is good, wholesome and lovely. Are there thoughts we might want to say sorry to God about?
- Eyes – how is our seeing? Do we look at people judgmentally, or as objects of desire, rather than as children of God made in God's image?
- Ears – how is our hearing? Are we deaf to the needs of others around us? Christians spend time listening to God, especially as they read the Bible. How is our listening?
- Mouth – in the letter of James in the Bible we are warned that though the tongue is small, it can do a lot of harm. How is our speaking? Paul says in the letter to the Ephesians, 'Let nothing unwholesome come out of your mouth but only what is good for building others up.' Do we need to say sorry for something we have said?
- Heart – how are our hearts? Do we have any heart problems? Are we loving and kind to those around us? Do we need to have a look at our hearts over Lent?
- Hands – can get us into all sorts of trouble. We have a choice as to how to use our hands. We can use them to help or to fight, to show care or to abuse, to work hard or to be idle. Have we used our hands as we should?
- Feet – our feet take us where we want to go. It may be that we need to think about whether we have been going in the right direction. Have we been following the crowd or going the right way?

(You don't have to cover all these body parts – you may want to focus on one or two.)

5. Congratulate the patient – s/he has passed the medical. Over the rest of Lent, think about these parts of our bodies and see whether they are as healthy on the inside as they look on the outside.

Time for reflection

Heavenly Father,
Thank you that you designed us perfectly
to be created in your image.
We are sorry that so often we have failed
to use our bodies in the way that you want us to.
Help us in this season of Lent to value ourselves and each
   other
so that we demonstrate your love
in all that we say, in all that we are and in all that we do;
in Jesus' name.
Amen.

 Song

'God knows me' (*Come and Praise*, 15)

HERE BE DRAGONS –
ST GEORGE'S DAY

By Stuart Kerner

Suitable for Key Stage Three

Aim

To consider the story of St George and dragons in our own lives.

Preparation and materials

- An English flag, or something bearing St George's cross.
- Bible reading: Revelation 12.9–17.

Assembly

1. Ask your audience who the patron saint of England is; hopefully you will receive the correct answer that it is St George. Show the England flag and comment that the red cross is actually the cross of St George.
2. Say that St George is of course most famous for slaying a dragon. But what is a dragon and do dragons really exist?
3. Tell them that Webster's Dictionary says that the word dragon comes to us from the Greek for serpent or snake and is a fabulous animal usually represented as a monstrous, winged creature with scaly skin, a crested head and enormous claws.
4. Say that you may be surprised to know that real dragons do still exist: the water dragon is a popular small lizard often kept as a pet, and the Komodo dragon (whose existence was not confirmed until the early 1900s!) is the largest known lizard, reaching lengths of 3 metres (10 feet), and weighing about 68 kilograms (150 pounds). Its bright yellow tongue

could be mistaken for a flame, while its vicious nature would scare anyone away.

5. Admit that these are really just big lizards rather than actual dragons.

6. Comment that the best place to find dragons is in fairytales and legends where a dragon's main function is as an accessory to show off the bravery of the knight challenging him. But to Christians the dragon is something else.

7. The famous story in which St George saved a young woman by slaying a dragon is unlikely to be based on fact, even if we say that the dragon may have been a crocodile, as some Orthodox Christians claim.

8. The story is almost certainly a metaphor for the rescue of the Church from persecution and the triumph of innocence over evil, the princess representing the Church, and the dragon, Satan. The dragon as a Christian symbol of evil comes to us from the book of Revelation – the final book of the Bible. Revelation 12.9 says: 'The great dragon was thrown down, that serpent of old that led the whole world astray, whose name is Satan or the Devil'; and in Psalm 91.13 the psalmist writes, 'The dragon shall God trample under foot.'

9. Today's hymn has the line '... giants have fled, and the knights are no more and the dragons are dead.' If only they were! There *are* still dragons all around us – only not of the scaly variety. These 'dragons', which stalk the planet, crushing whole nations and communities in their path, are poverty, debt, warfare, disease; and there are smaller 'dragons' that lurk in our minds and in our hearts – things in our lives that we personally have to conquer – fear, hatred, guilt and envy.

10. Comment that all of us have 'dragons' in our lives – something which we fear above all else. For some people it is exams that they must battle against; for others it is staying out of trouble; and for still others it is bullying that has to be combated. What are *your* dragons?

Time for reflection

We think of the dragons in the world: war, violence, fear,
  poverty and starvation ...
We think of the dragons in our own lives: greed, hatred, guilt
  and worry ...
We must put on the armour of courage,
we must take up the sword of truth,
we must accept the shield of justice
to help us wipe out these evils.

Let us today resolve to slay these dragons.

> Father,
> Give us the courage of St George
> to stand up for what is right and good.
> Give us the compassion of St George
> to help those in need.
> Give us the faith of St George
> to lead a righteous life.
> **Amen.**

 ## Song

'When a knight won his spurs' (*Come and Praise*, 50)

FLUFFY BUNNIES ARE OPTIONAL – EASTER

By Stuart Kerner

Suitable for Key Stage Three

 Aim

To explain the concept of the atonement.

 Preparation and materials

- Examples of 'non-religious' Easter cards.
- One large and some small Easter eggs (cream eggs are ideal).
- A willing helper who is prepared to be bellowed at and act the victim.

 Assembly

1. Tell the audience that you recently went shopping for Easter cards. Unfortunately, all you found were ones with pictures of fluffy bunnies and cute yellow chicks, but very few with anything connected with Easter (show examples of cards).
2. Comment that for Christians all these sweet and cuddly images fail to reflect the true spirit of Easter, which involves scenes of absolute horror and torture when Jesus was crucified on the day we call Good Friday, and the story of the greatest event in human history when he rose again on Easter Day.
3. Say that at the heart of Easter is Jesus completing his mission: to die for all our sins, and then go one better and beat death entirely through resurrection. Christians call this 'the atonement' – when God and humanity resolved their differences and God put all the sins committed by human beings behind them.

4. Tell the audience that you will demonstrate what it was that Jesus did when he bore our sins on the cross. Ask them to imagine that the whole assembly have done something unspeakably wrong: perhaps they all took part in a food fight in the canteen, or they all talked during a speech given by an important visitor.

5. Say that they all deserve to be punished, but you will take out your anger and frustration on just one 'sacrificial lamb'. Look around the audience until you fix your eyes on your prepared 'victim'. Tell them in no uncertain terms to stand up, and then shout at them as loudly and as viciously as you can before sending them out of the hall.

6. Now say that because everyone else's guilt has been taken away by the scapegoat, you can give the rest of them a treat. (Carefully) throw the small Easter eggs into the audience, and smile radiantly to show your approval.

7. Ask your victim to come back in and present them with the large Easter egg as a reward, before sending them back to their seat with a well-earned round of applause.

8. Comment that at Easter we should remember the essentials, namely, that, like your assembly scapegoat, Jesus removed our sins (through his crucifixion), before returning with the greater prize: victory over death and life eternal. Fluffy bunnies are optional!

 Time for reflection

The following quotations could be used to put the life and importance of Christ in context:

> All the armies that ever marched, and all the navies that ever were built, and all the parliaments that ever sat, and all the kings that ever reigned, put together, have not affected the life of man upon this earth as powerfully as has this one solitary life.
>
> *Malcolm Muggeridge (1903–90)*

> God has himself gone through the whole of human experience, from the trivial irritations of family life and the cramping restrictions of hard work and lack of money

to the worst horrors of pain and humiliation, defeat, despair, and death.

Dorothy L. Sayers (1893–1957)

Alexander, Caesar, Charlemagne, and myself founded empires; but upon what did we rest the creations of our genius? Upon force. Jesus Christ alone founded his empire upon love, and at this hour millions of men would die for him.

Napoleon Bonaparte (1769–1821)

Lord Jesus,
When you opened your arms on the cross,
you embraced us all.
When you died on the cross,
you gave us all new life.
When you rose again,
you conquered death.
Let us give thanks this Eastertide
for your wonderful sacrifice.
Amen.

 Song

'Lord of the dance' (*Come and Praise*, 22)

THE FIRE OF PENTECOST

By Charlotte Benstead

Suitable for Key Stage Three

Aim

To reflect on God's gifts of forgiveness and love at Pentecost.

Preparation and materials

- It would be very useful (if health and safety will allow) to have a small, contained fire or, failing that, a candle with a strong flame.
- Bible reading: Acts 2.1–21.
- Suggested music: 'Firestarter' by The Prodigy; 'Fire' by The Crazy World of Arthur Brown.

Assembly

1. Begin by showing the audience your fire or candle. Ask them to consider how amazing an elemental force fire is. Comment that for many people, fire holds both fascination and fear.
2. Say that human beings have been gathering around fire ever since we learned to harness its power as cave-dwellers many, many millennia ago. Without the heat of fire on our bodies, its ability to cook our food, ward off predators and banish the darkness, we would have died out long since.
3. Of course, fire is not always our friend. Fire, out of control, destroys. House fires and forest fires, for example, bring tragedy to the lives of millions of people each year.
4. In medieval times people were terrified by fire, and not just the fire that could destroy their wooden houses, but also the flames of hell. Hell was thought to be a place of eternal

punishment and suffering where evil people met their fate of fire and torture.

5. Although Jesus talked more of hell than heaven, he offered love and forgiveness. Even when he was on the cross, Jesus refused to condemn those who were torturing and killing him. Instead, he forgave them, and he promised Paradise, not hell, to the thief dying next to him.

6. For most Christians the kind of fire Jesus brings is to be found at Pentecost.

7. Read Acts 2.1–21.

8. If you have ever seen a blacksmith at work, perhaps on television, you will know the effect that fire has on iron and steel: it *purifies*, it *converts* and it *strengthens*. In other words, it totally transforms a humble piece of metal into something strong and beautiful.

9. At Pentecost we are reminded that God's fire has exactly the same effect. The fire of Pentecost can totally transform a person's life.

 ## Time for reflection

The fire

One day I saw a fire
All red and gold and blue,
And as the fire came nearer
I wondered what to do.

It didn't seem to threaten.
It just stood there all ablaze,
And as the fire stared at me
I met its potent gaze.

I sought to find its purpose,
It trembled for a bit.
Then it seemed to speak to me,
Words filled with sense and wit.

'Stand up for all your principles.
Be as strong willed as you can.
Always speak your mind, don't lie,
And respect your fellow man.'

As the fire grew dimmer
I swear it seemed to smile.
Then it slowly died away
But its words remained awhile.

If you see this fire
Don't fear its smoke and heat,
Listen closely to it:
It will make your life complete.

Stuart Kerner

Father,
At Pentecost you touched the followers of Jesus with tongues
    of fire.
Fill us with the fire of your Spirit:
let us feel the heat of your love,
light us up with your peace,
consume our selfish desires,
and convert us into models of righteousness.
Amen.

 Song

'Spirit of God' (*Come and Praise*, 63)

EXAMS

By Stuart Kerner

Suitable for whole school

 Aim

To encourage students to keep exam stress in proportion.

 Preparation and materials

- OHP transparency with some of the exam 'howlers' (see point 4).

 Assembly

1. Children in England are the most tested in the world. According to the *Times Educational Supplement*, it is estimated that they will undertake up to 105 tests and exams during their school years. These include SATs – optional and compulsory – GCSEs, NVQs, GNVQs, modular and vocational A Levels, as well as a whole range of class tests, including CATs, baseline assessments, reading, listening, language and IQ tests.
2. One headteacher worked out that students are out of lessons for at least 46 weeks in the course of their seven-year secondary careers and spend 150 hours actually sitting exams.
3. As a result of the pressure this creates, Childline estimates that it receives 800 calls a year from pupils suffering from exam stress, some of them as young as nine years old. Also the annual cost of exams and tests has increased to more than £200 million – a 50 per cent rise since 1997.
4. And to make matters worse, after all the stress, anxiety, effort and sleepless nights, when the results come in, the media tell us that exams are getting easier!

5. Some people find exams easier than others. Here are some examples of real answers given by exam candidates who perhaps didn't do very well (you can use as few or as many as you feel appropriate):

When you smell an odourless gas, it is probably carbon monoxide.

A super saturated solution is one that holds more than it can hold.

Before giving a blood transfusion, find out if the blood is affirmative or negative.

Blood flows down one leg and up the other.

Christians go on pilgrimage to Lord's.

Dew is formed on leaves when the sun shines down on them and makes them perspire.

For a nosebleed: Put the nose much lower than the body until the heart stops.

Magnet: Something you find crawling all over a dead cat.

Momentum: What you give a person when they are going away.

Mushrooms always grow in damp places and so they look like umbrellas.

The moon is a planet just like the earth, only it is even deader.

The skeleton is what is left after the insides have been taken out and the outsides have been taken off.

The purpose of the skeleton is something to hitch meat to.

The tides are a fight between the Earth and moon. All water tends towards the moon, because there is no water in the moon, and nature abhors a vacuum. I forget where the sun joins in this fight.

To keep milk from turning sour: Keep it in the cow.

To remove dust from the eye, pull the eye down over the nose.

A Christian man should have only one wife. This is called monotony.

A fossil is an extinct animal. The older it is, the more extinct it is.

Jesus was born because his mother Mary had an immaculate contraption.

Lot's wife was a pillar of salt by day and a ball of fire by night.

Moses went to the top of Mount Cyanide to get the 10 Commandments.

Name the four seasons: Salt, mustard, pepper, vinegar.

Noah's wife was Joan of Ark.

One of the opossums was St Matthew.

Solomon had 100 wives and 700 porcupines.

The epistles were the wives of the apostles.

The first book of the Bible is Guinness's in which Adam and Eve were created from an apple.

The Jewish people had trouble throughout their history with unsympathetic Genitals.

The people who followed Jesus were called the 12 decibels.

The seventh commandment is, Thou shalt not admit adultery.

What is a co-operative? It's a kind of shop that is not as dear as places like Marks and Spencer.

What is Britain's highest award for valour in war? Nelson's Column.

What's a Hindu? It lays eggs.

6. But do we really need all these these tests and exams? Does being bad at exams make us failures? God clearly doesn't think so. The Bible has numerous examples of people having tests set by God, many of whom were abject failures.

- Adam and Eve in Genesis 3 were tested by God in the Garden of Eden. They, of course, failed, but God didn't give up on them.
- Job was tested by Satan, he passed with flying colours.
- When they were in the wilderness, the people of Israel were tested by God for 40 years (see Deuteronomy 8.15–16). All but two of them failed, and they died in the wilderness. But their grown-up children went on to enter the promised land.
- Jesus at the beginning of his ministry was tested by Satan and passed all three of his exams (Luke 4.1–13).

- The testing of Simon Peter after the arrest of Jesus is another good example. He failed at his first attempt, but later passed, and went on to better things (Mark 14.29–31, 66–72).

7. In some of these examples, those who were failures went on to achieve greatness because they trusted in God and persevered. Above all, they tried.

8. Finish with this story to illustrate the idea that exams are more a test of character than anything else:

A college professor stood before his class of 20 biology students, about to hand out the final exam.

'I want to say that it's been a pleasure teaching you this term. I know you've all worked extremely hard and many of you are off to medical school after the summer holiday.

'So that no one gets their overall grades messed up because they might have been celebrating a bit too much this week, anyone who would like to opt out of the final exam today will receive a B for the course.'

There was much rejoicing among the class as students got up, passed by the professor to thank him and sign out on his offer. As the last taker left the room, the professor looked out over the handful of remaining students and asked, 'Anyone else? This is your last chance.'

One final student rose up and took the offer.

The professor closed the door and took attendance of those students remaining. 'I'm glad to see you believe in yourself,' he said. 'You all have As.'

 Time for reflection

Lord,
It seems as though our lives are one test after another,
weighing us in somebody's balance.
Save us from taking the coming tests too seriously or too
    lightly,
but grant that we may reflect the best of the work we've done
and the best of the teaching we've received;
through Jesus Christ our Lord.
Amen.

Song

'The wise may bring their learning' (*Come and Praise*, 64)

ROOM FOR IMPROVEMENT? REPORTS

By Joanne Sincock

Suitable for Key Stage Three

Aim

To reflect on school reports and how you can change your future for the better.

Preparation and materials

None required.

Assembly

1. This is the time of year when your teachers are busy writing your end of year report. This can be a difficult task for many teachers who may have to write hundreds of reports in a very short space of time. Trying to think of something original to say is quite hard, especially when they have to talk about students who may not have done very well.
2. For many school students this can be a very worrying time. How have I done this year? Have I improved on last year? What will my parents say when they read my report?
3. Of course, these feelings are nothing new. For several hundred years children have dreaded the annual summary of their work, effort and behaviour.
4. In the opening chapter of *Matilda* by Roald Dahl, the author describes how parents sometimes think that their child's achievements are at the level of genius. Dahl, puzzled by such 'twaddle', counsels teachers to resort to foul play when writing reports. He suggests they write that a child with limited ability is 'a total washout'. Dahl implies that if he were a teacher, he would enjoy writing the end-of-term reports for the bad children in his class.

5. Here are some real reports written about famous people. See if you can guess to whom they belong:

Certainly on the road to failure ... hopeless ... rather a clown in class ... wasting other pupils' time.
(Of one of the most successful musicians of all time: Beatle, John Lennon)

Is a constant trouble to everybody and is always in some scrape or other. He cannot be trusted to behave himself anywhere. He has no ambition ...
(Of Sir Winston Churchill: voted by television viewers the greatest Briton of all time)

I have never met a boy who so persistently writes the exact opposite of what he means. He seems incapable of organizing his thoughts on paper!
(Of Roald Dahl: some say the most popular children's author ever)

6. These comments are all pretty harsh, and we will never know if they were really deserved. We do know, however, that in later life these three men all achieved great things.
7. Perhaps this means that there is hope for students who receive even the most awful school report. Maybe, through hard work and perseverance, by never giving up and by completing our daily tasks to the very best of our abilities, we will achieve our true potential.

 Time for reflection

What sort of report do you hope to get?
What sort of report do you think you deserve?
What sort of report do you think you *will* get?

Whatever your report includes, resolve to always:

work hard
do your best,
and *never, ever* give up.

Dear Lord,
We hate being judged and found wanting.
Help us to ensure that we always give our best,
always try our hardest,
and always strive to achieve.
Amen.

 Song

'Lord of all hopefulness' (*Come and Praise*, 52)

EDUCATION – END OF THE SCHOOL YEAR

By Stuart Kerner

Suitable for Key Stage Three

Aim

To reflect on our attitudes to schooling and education.

Preparation and materials

- Bible reading: Proverbs 3.13–18.
- Suggested music: 'Baggy Trousers' by Madness; 'Schooldays' by The Kinks.

Assembly

1. Each morning during term time you set off for school. Some of you may be pleased to come and look forward to what you are going to do during the day; others of you may wish that you could stay at home instead.
2. However you may feel about school, unless you receive home tuition, you have to attend, because it's the law that all young people must be educated.
3. If you had lived 150 years ago, you would possibly have loved the chance to learn at an institution like this because only a few children had the opportunity. In fact, many children had to go out to work before they were as old as you are now. Indeed, most of you would have probably been working long, tiring hours in a mill or at some other trade.
4. However, in 1870 a law was passed that laid down that schools were to be provided for all children between the ages of 5 and 13. School Boards were set up to build the schools

that were necessary. Since then schools have been built wherever they were needed.

5. Have you ever heard the saying that schooldays are the happiest days of your life? Do you agree with this saying? (You might take a show of hands – probably not many!)

6. Those of you who disagree might be interested to know that an actor called Robert Morley responded to this saying with the words: 'Show me the man who has enjoyed his schooldays and I will show you a bully and a bore!'

7. It is likely that whoever first said it was probably an adult! It seems that for most young people the idea that life doesn't get better than this must be something of a worry! Paul Merton, from TV's *Have I Got News For You,* said, 'My schooldays were the happiest days of my life; which should give you some indication of the misery I've endured over the past 25 years.'

8. But is school really that bad? Surely there are some positive aspects.

9. The memories of fun, friendships, fights, fears, failures, fashions and first love will leave a lasting impression in your heart that years from now will cause you to chuckle and bring a tear to your eye.

10. Today we have greater opportunities than ever before, but it is up to each one of us to make the most of them – to be conscientious in our work so that we may learn all we can; to learn when to give and take and how to live with others; and to obtain for ourselves wisdom and understanding.

11. An Old Testament writer tells of the value of wisdom and understanding:

God blesses everyone who has wisdom and understanding.
Wisdom is worth more than silver; it makes you much richer
   than gold.
Wisdom is more valuable than precious jewels;
nothing you want compares with her.
In her right hand Wisdom holds a long life,
and in her left hand are wealth and honour.
Wisdom makes life pleasant and leads us safely along.

Proverbs 3.13–18

Time for reflection

I remember going to school, and although there were *so* many times I didn't enjoy school and wish I didn't have to go, sometimes now I wish I could go back. Not for the friends, but just for the chance to read interesting books and learn new things.

In some countries young people wish they could go to school, but they cannot, they have to go to work so that they have enough money to eat.

Believe me; you would rather go to school than go to work. I remember thinking when I was young that work would be just as hard as school, but I grew up and found out I was wrong.

Sometimes I miss school.

Written by a 30-year-old mother of three

Dear God,
Bless our school and all who come here every day.
Bless our teachers and those who clean our school and keep it
     warm,
and those who prepare and serve our meals.
May we be strong to tackle hard and unpleasant tasks,
loyal to our friends and forgiving to our enemies;
through Jesus Christ our Lord.
Amen.

 Song

'One more step' (*Come and Praise*, 47)

How to Live

WISHING YOUR LIFE AWAY

by Helen Swain

Suitable for Key Stage Three

Aim

To encourage the sensible use of time.

Preparation and materials

- You might like to prepare the Latin inscriptions *carpe diem* and *tempus fugit* on a large sheet of paper or an OHP transparency.
- Bible reading: Ecclesiastes 3.1–8.

Assembly

1. Introduce the assembly by asking students what they did over the weekend. To encourage a varied response, you could make suggestions: went to the match, the pictures, perhaps to church, to a party, or maybe just stayed in and watched TV.
2. Now ask about what they are looking forward to doing next weekend.
3. Say that people often spend time discussing their plans for their days off, and you can understand this sort of conversation about days off work and days off school. School takes up a lot of time on weekdays. There's the normal timetable, perhaps some sporting fixture or club after school and not much space for anything but homework between your evening meal and bedtime.
4. But the weekend gives us two clear days – so it's no wonder we talk about our leisure plans and look forward to Friday when we can begin to do what we want to do instead of whatever someone else tells us to do.

5. There's only one problem with looking forward to something special: it can encourage us almost to live our lives in the future. And the only thing wrong with that is it takes away our enjoyment of the present.

6. Once a Christian man called Augustine prayed, 'Lord, make me good, but not just yet.' He prayed like that because he was having such a good time and he didn't want the fun to stop. Of course, the present isn't always enjoyable. Sometimes you might think it's hardly bearable. So looking forward to a treat in the future – like a holiday or a film – can help us when we feel a bit depressed.

7. But living in the future isn't really living at all. It's just making pictures in your imagination. The present – what a religious writer by the name of Paul Tillich called 'the eternal now' – is all we've got. Our lives are a lot richer when we try to appreciate what's happening at this very moment in time.

8. Our lives are made up of tiny moments and each one is important. We can spend each moment doing the right thing or the wrong thing.

9. If we squander our hours, ruin our days and throw away our weeks, our lives will be empty. But if we see each hour as an opportunity, if we spend each day in growing and if we use each week to move ahead, our lives will be full.

10. In the film *Dead Poets Society*, Robin Williams plays a teacher called John Keating who tries to give his students an appreciation of how amazing life is, and yet how short it can be. Mr Keating introduces his students to two ideas, usually expressed in Latin: *tempus fugit* – 'time flies' and *carpe diem* – 'seize the day'.

11. *Dead Poets Society* reminds us to seize each day and to cherish it dearly, as we can never stop the endless flow of time. In order to avoid missed chances or regrets in later life we must always try to make our lives amazing, and do it *now*!

12. You might want to incorporate this story into your assembly to demonstrate the need for using time wisely:

One day Satan was discussing with another devil how they could do more evil in the world.

'One thing you will soon realize,' said Satan. 'Human

beings are very good at doing terrible things – all they need is a little encouragement.'

'Why don't we spread the word that there is no God, then?' asked the other devil.

'No, no, they wouldn't believe that.'

The second devil thought for a while. Then he came up with another idea. 'Why don't we spread the rumour that there's no hell? That will give them plenty of opportunity for doing wrong without any need to worry about it.'

Satan shook his head. 'Human beings are not stupid. But your suggestions have given me a good idea. Go to earth and remind everyone that there is a God and then remind them that there is hell too. But then tell them not to worry as they have plenty of time before they need concern themselves about either. Then you'll see what trouble they can get into!'

13. Read Ecclesiastes 3.1–8.

 Time for reflection

Let's think of those who look back and wish they had an extra day, or more time:

- people who don't have enough time for what they are expected to do;
- people who have lost a sense of balance and proportion in their lives;
- people who feel that they have made a mess of everything and would like to be able to start again.

We think, too, about those who might wish for less time:

- people who are worried about what might happen;
- people who are in despair;
- people who suffer hours of pain and illness;
- people who are in prison or are being tortured;
- people who wish to die.

Let us resolve to use the time we have wisely, and take advantage of the opportunities we have.

Dear God,
Teach us to use our time wisely.
Help us to fill each second.
Help us to take advantage of each minute.
Help us to make the most of each hour.
And, above all, give us the wisdom to seize each day.
Amen.

 Song

'This is the day the Lord has made' (*Mission Praise*, 691)

ACTIONS SPEAK LOUDER THAN WORDS

By Helen Lycitt

Suitable for Whole School

Aim

To help students consider the importance of showing commitment and acting on their beliefs.

Preparation and materials

- A tin of fruit or other dessert (e.g. chocolate rice pudding) with the label removed and replaced with a dog food label, a tin-opener, a fork.
- Music: *Chariots of Fire* theme by Vangelis.
- There are two stories below, both of which can be used, depending on the time available.
- A dramatized version of one of the stories about Blondin is available at <http://www.dramatix.org/Evangelism/blondin.html>.

Assembly

1. Appear rushed and unprepared, and apologise to students that you have been held up (in traffic, etc.). Ask them if they mind you having your breakfast while doing assembly.
2. Produce your tin of 'dog food' (actually a tin of fruit or other dessert), open it and proceed to take a mouthful. Wait for reactions.
3. Students should be appalled and you can play up to this by looking surprised, hurt, embarrassed, etc. Tell the audience that it's actually quite nice and they shouldn't knock it until they've tried it. Then, as if it has occurred to you that it may

seem a little strange, ask if there's anyone in the audience who doesn't believe that it really is dog food. Ask for a show of hands.

4. Say to those with their hands up, 'Who is prepared to put their money where their mouth is and try some?' (The number of hands should drop dramatically!)

5. Get a volunteer to come up to the front to try it. Make them close their eyes and then give them some on a spoon. Say, 'Open you eyes and tell everyone what it tastes like.' When they have confirmed that it isn't dog food, thank them for their courage and ensure they get a round of applause.

6. Tell the following story to illustrate the point further:

> Charles Blondin was one of the world's greatest funambulists (that's a tightrope walker to you), and on 15 September 1860 he performed one of the most amazing stunts the world has ever seen.
>
> Before a great crowd, Blondin walked a tightrope stretched across Niagara Falls in Canada. The tightrope was 49 metres (160 feet) above the Falls, and it stretched for 335 metres (1,100 feet)across.
>
> After that, Blondin crossed over Niagara Falls on a tightrope many times. On one occasion he stopped in the middle and cooked an omelette.
>
> Another time he wheeled a wheelbarrow over the Falls. After Blondin had walked one way, he asked the crowd if they believed he could wheel a person across in a wheelbarrow. They all shouted 'Yes!' because he was the greatest tightrope walker in the world. So he then asked for a volunteer – but no one spoke up! No one was prepared to trust Blondin and put what they believed into practice.
>
> But one person did trust Blondin. He was Henry Colcord, Blondin's manager. On 17 August 1859 Blondin walked over the falls on a tightrope carrying Henry Colcord on his back. Colcord alone had real confidence and trust in Blondin's skill as a tightrope walker.

7. The crowd in this story all said they believed in the abilities of Blondin, but when they were challenged to do something about it no one moved. They weren't prepared to put their

belief into action! Every day people say they believe in things but are these beliefs important enough to do something about? Perhaps we genuinely do believe, but pressure from those around us – from our friends outside school, from our family, from our classmates – stops us from making a commitment.

8. Maybe you believed it was important to revise hard for your exams, but your friends persuaded you against it. Perhaps you believe it is important to help and support younger students, but pressure from others has led you into bullying.

9. Arrange for the theme from *Chariots of Fire* to be played and ask if anyone knows where it comes from. Then say that you want to tell them about a man who had the courage to stand by his beliefs and act on them.

Say that *Chariots of Fire* is a film which includes the story of Eric Liddell, a Scottish athlete, born in 1902, who in the 1924 Olympics earned the nickname the 'Flying Scotsman'.

Liddell was born in China, the son of a Scottish missionary. He was educated at Eltham College and Edinburgh University, where his outstanding speed earned him seven caps in the Scotland rugby team.

He was selected to represent Great Britain in the 100 metres at the 1924 Olympics in Paris. He would have been the favourite to win the event, as he was regarded as one of the world's greatest sprinters. But Eric refused to take part in the event. Not because he was injured. Not because he thought he couldn't win. But because the heats were to be run on a Sunday.

Eric Liddell was a Christian who believed that it was wrong to do any activity on a Sunday except worship God. He held this belief so strongly that he was prepared to give up this great opportunity at the Olympics.

At the last minute, Liddell entered the 200 and 400 metre events, where he was considered to have little or no chance. However, to everyone's amazement Liddell took the bronze medal in the final of the 200 metres, and went on to win the gold medal in the 400 metres, in a world record time of 47.6 seconds.

Eric Liddell's courage to stand by his beliefs was rewarded with amazing success. He believed that God was with him, guiding him. Later Eric followed in his father's footsteps and became a missionary in China.

The 1981 film *Chariots of Fire*, which tells the story of Eric Liddell's athletic triumphs, won the Oscar for the best film of the Year.

Eric Liddell had a strong belief. He showed commitment to that belief, and his courage and faith paid off.

 Time for reflection

Let us think about what we believe and whether we act on our beliefs or allow others to influence us to compromise those beliefs.

Lord,
Let us not be ashamed to stand up for what we believe.
When others laugh at us,
or try to make us feel foolish,
give us the courage of our convictions.
Help us always to follow the right path.
Amen.

 Song

'Stand up! stand up for Jesus' (*Mission Praise*, 617)

RISE TO THE CHALLENGE

By Stuart Kerner

Suitable for Key Stage Three

 Aim

To encourage spiritual discipline and effort, through the analogy of an athlete.

 Preparation and materials

- You might like to dress in a tracksuit and trainers or some other sporting outfit.
- Bible reading: 1 Corinthians 9.24–27.

 Assembly

1. Ask the students how many of them followed the 2006 Olympics in Athens (or a recent sporting event).
2. Talk about the achievements of the athletes. Discuss the amount of preparation undertaken by each competitor. Similar strenuous training was known to people around the time of Jesus.
3. St Paul, author of many of the letters in the New Testament, wrote the following passage about the training of an athlete. His readers were Christians living in the Greek city of Corinth.

Do you not know that in a race all the runners run, but only one gets the prize? Run in such a way as to get the prize. Everyone who competes in the games goes into strict training. They do it to get a crown that will not last; but we do it to get a crown that will last for ever. Therefore I do not run like a man running aimlessly; I do not fight like a man beating the air. No, I beat my body and make it my slave so that after I have preached to others, I myself will not be disqualified for the prize.

1 Corinthians 9.24–27

4. The good runner keeps looking forward towards the finishing line. That's where he focuses his attention. As Christians we should also be looking towards the finishing line. Our goal is to live close to Jesus and to do things his way.

5. In life we need determination to succeed and we have to take strict control of ourselves as we train for the future. We are also wise if we listen to our 'coach' – none other than God – whose words come to us in all sorts of ways.

6. Whereas the physical athlete endures much (change in diet, bodily exhaustion, and mental discipline) in the hope that he or she will one day be considered 'the best', an honour which sadly is often soon forgotten, the spiritual athlete also suffers great hardship (fasting, prayer, as well as other physical and spiritual disciplines), not for earthly glory, but for the unending reward of heaven. He welcomes discipline and training for a spiritual reward. This is the 'well done' of Jesus and the unending glory of heaven.

  If you are constrained by time you might prefer to conclude the assembly here; if you have more time you may wish to continue.

7. People who are willing to suffer great hardship (fasting, prayer, as well as other spiritual and physical disciplines) are called 'ascetics', a word that comes from a Greek word meaning 'exercise'. One such Christian ascetic was called Simeon the Stylite. A 'stylite' was someone who, believe it or not, spent their life at the top of a stone pillar.

8. Simeon was born at Sisan, near the northern border of Syria, and began life as a shepherd boy looking after his father's flock of sheep.

9. When he was 13 years old, he heard the gospel passage, 'Blessed are they who mourn; blessed are the clean of heart.' He went to a wise old man and asked him the meaning of these words. This man explained to the boy that eternal happiness can only be gained by suffering, and is best

achieved by isolation. Impressed with this explanation, the young man joined a nearby monastery.

10. After some years in different monasteries, Simeon began to live alone. In order to avoid the many visitors who were constantly seeking him out, he decided to live on the top of a pillar. For most of the time he stood on the pillar, exposed to all kinds of weather, and absorbed in non-stop prayer. He died in 459 at the age of 69, having lived 36 years of his life on the top of different pillars.

11. After Simeon's death, pilgrims continued to flock to the site of his last pillar, and in 472 building began on a great basilica in Syria. Its ruins still remain today and contain what is left of the pillar.

12. Simeon's life was extraordinary from many points of view. Actually, to stand as he did on the top of a pillar was to make himself into a kind of statue. It is a position that many proud people might like to assume in order to be admired. But this was not the case with St Simeon, who left the monastery to avoid the many visitors who constantly tried to see him.

13. You can see that his life was inspired by an incredible faith. He was focused entirely on constant meditation of God. His life was entirely exposed, almost without a moment of privacy. He could be seen by anyone who wanted to look at him – a bit like the contestants in *Big Brother*.

14. His example of continuous prayer encouraged others to lead simple, more disciplined lives – to look for solitude and abandon earthly things.

15. Far from seeking it out, many people today try to escape from silence and solitude. We like to be with others all day long. When we're alone, we break the solitude by turning on the radio, or TV, or our Gameboys. We treat our houses, not as places to think and consider, but just as places to eat, drink and sleep before running out again.

16. Just as the Olympic athletes practise discipline and train themselves for great achievements, we too should strive for excellence. Do we live our lives without ever thinking too much about higher things? The New Testament does not teach that all everyday things are harmful – far from it – but some are! What, in our lives, should we seek to 'rise above'?

Time for reflection

Close your eyes and imagine you have trained for an important race.

See yourself on the course ... noticing the spectators, the environment ... you are getting ready for the race ... you are in your shorts ... your number is pinned to your chest ... People are all around. Imagine the sounds and feel the energy about you and within you. You do your warm-up routine. You line up, feeling the excitement in your body, hearing the instructions. The starting pistol makes a loud, piercing 'crack' ... you're off ... your legs feel good, they're loose and warm and ready to go ... you begin to loosen up all over ... warming up ... breathing hard and deeply ... your body ... settles into its rhythm ... you feel marvellous ... after all your preparation this feels easy to you. You become aware of the track under your feet and the sound your strides make ... you run hard and with ease ... you are an excellent runner and this is an easy race for you. You see the finishing tape up ahead ... you're passing some other runners now ... in complete control ... you press on ... surging ... passing ... accelerating ... you sprint the last 200 metres ... passing more runners ... taking them by surprise ... you cross the finishing line ... the first across the line ... you gasp for breath ...sides heaving; ... breathing hard ... tired ... exhilarated ... excited ... joyful. Feel the elation rising in your body ... the joy, the pleasure. You have achieved your goals ... experience it all in your body ... thanking your body for all it has given you today. Let it all flow through you ... in every blood vessel and every cell ... feel the satisfaction, the confidence, the sense of achievement ... hear the crowd ... your friends and those you don't know ... experience it all. You are a winner!

Now open your eyes and take that feeling of a job well done with you in all you do today.

Help us, Lord, to be successful in life.
Help us to control our minds, our bodies and our actions.
Help us to listen for your words of guidance and inspiration;
and so make us real champions in all we strive to achieve.
Amen.

Hymn

'Fight the good fight' (*Mission Praise*, 143)

A STRANGER IS A FRIEND YOU HAVEN'T MADE YET

By Stuart Kerner

Suitable for Whole School

Aim

To realize the need to extend friendship to all, especially to people we don't really know or like.

Preparation and materials

- You might like to copy the poem on to an OHP transparency.
- The story of the demoniac can be found in Luke 8.26–39.
- This assembly could be used in connection with issues involving refugees or asylum seekers.

Assembly

1. Tell the students you want to read them part of a poem by Walter Alexander Raleigh (1861–1922) entitled 'Wishes of an elderly man wished at a garden party, June 1914'.

   I wish I loved the human race;
   I wish I loved its silly face;
   I wish I liked the way it walks;
   I wish I liked the way it talks;
   And when I'm introduced to one,
   I wish I thought 'What Jolly Fun!'

2. Ask your audience if they have ever felt like the author, whether at a family party, travelling on a crowded bus or train in the rush hour, or in the waiting room of the doctor's surgery, surrounded by miserable patients sharing their germs.

3. We rarely admit, even to ourselves, that our attitude towards our fellow human beings is anything other than positive. If we're honest, however, the truth is that though we like some people enormously, and dislike a few with equal force, our attitude towards most people wavers between indifference and mistrust.

4. How can we know for certain that the person we can hear coming up behind us in the street isn't planning to steal our mobile phone? And when the phone rings everyone knows that the unknown person on the other end of the line, from the moment she opens her mouth is going to try to sell us something, probably double-glazing or insurance.

5. In the New Testament St Luke tells the story of Jesus healing a man possessed by demons. At the time of Jesus, people generally believed that most forms of illness were caused by wicked demons as a punishment for some kind of sin. This particular man sounds as if he was a pretty terrifying example of humanity. He was often seen running around stark naked and was constantly making strange noises day and night.

6. Now one might expect that the locals would be only too glad to see him cured, and grateful to Jesus for making this possible. But they weren't – far from it! They were afraid, and the whole crowd begged Jesus to leave them.

7. But what were they scared of? Well, judging from Luke's account, the miracle had been unusually dramatic and spectacular, which might partly account for the people's fear.

8. The real reason behind their panic might have been fear of having to form a new relationship with the former demoniac. Before Jesus turned up, they had ignored, disliked or perhaps made fun of him as a subhuman creature. Now he was standing in the midst of them clothed and in his right mind – every bit as human as they were!

9. How often do we reject people who are new to our school? How often are we reluctant to work with people outside our own friendship groups? How often have we been guilty of ignoring or making fun of people we don't really know?

10. When we leave school or go on work experience we have to get on with unknown people whether we like it or not.

Perhaps we should start to develop a more mature attitude today by taking notice of all those around us and remembering the saying, 'A stranger is a friend you haven't made yet.' Perhaps then our immediate reaction on being introduced to someone new would genuinely be, 'What jolly fun!'

 Time for reflection

Close your eyes.
Think of a time when you were new ...
Picture the scene in black and white ...
perhaps your first day at school.
Focus on how you felt ...

- scared?
- nervous?
- sick?
- lonely?

Now recall when you met a friend on that day ...
Imagine the friend in colour ...
Remember how it felt to be accepted.
As you feel the change in emotion, see the scene in full colour
    and concentrate on the feeling of being treated well.
Resolve to spread that feeling of warmth and love to
        everyone you meet today.

> Good Lord,
> Help us to be loving towards our neighbours,
> especially those who are unloved or unlovable.
> Let us spread the warmth of our friendship every day and at
>   every opportunity.
> **Amen.**

 Song

'Make me a channel of your peace' (*Mission Praise*, 153).

MR LAZY

By *Stuart Kerner*

Suitable for Whole School

Aim

To reflect on the unhealthy and spiritually damaging characteristic of laziness.

Preparation and materials

- Prepare an OHP transparency/PowerPoint slide of a sloth. There is a good image on <//bss.sfsu.edu/geog/bholzman/courses/fall99projects/sloth.htm> .
- You might also like to transfer the Bible quotes on to an OHP transparency (see point 3).
- Bible reading: Matthew 25.14–30.

Assembly

1. Show the picture of the sloth and ask if anyone knows what type of animal it is. Whatever the responses, inform the audience that this is a *Bradypus variegatus*, otherwise known as a brown-throated three-toed sloth.
2. Explain that the sloth is a slow-moving mammal that lives in trees in South America. Sloths spend most of their lives hanging upside down from tree branches; they eat, sleep, mate, and give birth suspended in the trees. They hold on to tree branches with the strong, curved claws on each of their four feet. Sloths are nocturnal. They sleep all day and are more active at night.

    The sloth got its name from its slow movement. It is not lazy, just slow-moving; the sloth is the slowest mammal on earth.

3. For Christians 'sloth' is one of the 'seven deadly sins', and refers to the sin of laziness and avoidance of work. The Bible has much to say on this matter, especially in the book of Proverbs:

> The lazy man turns over in bed. He gets no farther than a door swinging on its hinges.
>
> *Proverbs 26.14*

> Some people are too lazy to put food in their own mouths.
>
> *Proverbs 19.24*

> The lazy man stays at home; he says a lion might get him if he goes outside.
>
> *Proverbs 22.13*

> No matter how much a lazy man may want something, he will never get it. A hard worker will get everything he wants.
>
> *Proverbs 13.4*

> Never get a lazy man to do anything for you; he will be as irritating as vinegar on your teeth or smoke in your eyes.
>
> *Proverbs 10.26*

> Lazy people should learn a lesson from the way ants live. They have no leader, chief or ruler, but they store up their food during the summer, getting ready for the winter. How long is the lazy man going to lie in bed? When is he ever going to get up? 'I'll just take a short nap,' he says; 'I'll fold my hands and rest a while.' But while he sleeps, poverty will attack him like an armed robber.
>
> *Proverbs 6.6–11*

4. Does any of this apply to you? Listen to this story told by Jesus (read the parable of the talents from Matthew 25.14–30).
5. The silver coins in this story were called talents. In New Testament times, a 'talent' was a large sum of money. Because of this parable, its meaning has now changed. When we talk of talents today, we mean abilities that we are born

with, and are therefore God-given. The lazy servant wasted his talent through being slothful – does the same apply to you?

 Time for reflection

Dear Lord,
Help us to avoid being lazy.
Strengthen us to use our talents to their fullest,
and not waste opportunities through slothful living.
Amen.

 Song

'Stand up! stand up for Jesus' (*Mission Praise*, 211)

HONESTY

By Stuart Kerner

Suitable for Whole School

 Aim

To consider the need for honesty.

 Preparation and materials

- You might like to have a look at <www.spellingbee.com/>, the website of the National Spelling Bee.
- Have some colleagues on stand-by in case there are no volunteers.
- Two prizes for your mini-spelling bee (perhaps a pocket dictionary?).

 Assembly

1. Begin by asking your audience if anyone knows what a 'spelling bee' is. (You might refer to the film *Spellbound*, made in 2002, which followed eight American 14-year-olds as they set out to win the National Spelling Bee, or the BBC *Hardspell* series). In case anyone doesn't know, spelling bees are competitions, popular in the USA, in which children compete in spelling very hard words.
2. The first US National Spelling Bee was held in 1925, and was won by a young man called Frank Neuhauser who won by correctly spelling gladiolus, which is a type of flower.
3. Ask for two volunteers who think they are good at spelling. Hold a mini-spelling bee by alternately asking your competitors to spell the following words:

assembly	eight
arctic	asthma

| pharaoh | marriage |
| schizophrenic | pharmaceutical |

4. Give the winner a small prize and the loser a consolation prize and send them back to their seats with a well-earned round of applause.

5. Now tell your audience this true story from one of the national spelling contests:

> In the fourth round of the National Spelling Bee in Washington, eleven-year-old Rosalie Elliot from South Carolina was asked to spell the word 'avowal' – that's A-V-O-W-A-L.
>
> In her soft Southern accent she spelled it. But did she use an 'a' or an 'e' as the next to last letter? The judges couldn't decide.
>
> For several minutes they listened to tape playbacks, but the critical letter was blurred by her pronunciation.
>
> Eventually the chief judge put the question to the only person who knew the answer, little Rosalie. Surrounded by whispering young spellers, she now knew the correct spelling of the word.
>
> Without hesitating, she replied she had said 'e' and had misspelled it. As she walked silently from the stage, the entire audience stood and applauded. This must have been a proud moment for Rosalie's parents. Her honesty probably made them more proud of her than if she had won the entire competition.

6. You probably all know the saying, 'Honesty is the best policy', but consider what you would have done in the same circumstances.

7. The Bible has this to say on the subject of honesty: 'If you are good, you are guided by honesty. People who can't be trusted are destroyed by their own dishonesty' (Proverbs 11.3).

 Time for reflection

Tell the truth
Or tell a lie:

Better get an alibi!
Keep it straight
Or else conceal
All that's not completely real.

Liars fail to gain our trust,
Their golden words reduced to rust.
This advice still holds, you see:
Honesty's the best policy!
Stuart Kerner

Dear God,
When we are tempted to tell a lie,
keep us truthful.
When we are attracted by deceit,
keep us honest.
Give us the strength and courage
to avoid this and all other wrongdoing.
Amen.

 Song

'When a knight won his spurs' (*Come and Praise*, 50)

RULES

By Stuart Kerner

Suitable for Whole School

 Aim

To consider the need for rules.

 Preparation and materials

- An OHP transparency with your school rules.
- An OHP transparency with strange and stupid laws on it. You can find plenty of these at the following websites:
  www.dumblaws.com/
  http://tjshome.com/dumblaws.php
  www.lawguru.com/weird/

 Assembly

1. Begin by asking for a volunteer to tell you the school rules. When they have told you, show them on the OHP. Ask if anyone can explain the purpose of these rules. You should hopefully receive answers like 'to keep everyone safe', 'to maintain the reputation of the school' and 'to protect people and property'.
2. Ask what the effect of changing the rules might be. For instance, what if the Headteacher decided to make it a rule to wear only one sock on Thursdays, or that those students under five feet tall should be banned from playing football. The chances are people would disobey them.
3. Show the OHP with a selection of strange laws on. Ask if anyone can suggest reasons for these rules being made. You should hopefully receive some imaginative answers. Comment that even if we don't know the reason a rule is

put in place, or we don't agree with it, that does not mean we can choose to ignore it.

4. If a footballer decided the 'off-side rule' was useless, he couldn't just choose to disregard it. And if a driver considered the motorway speed limit outdated, he couldn't expect to get away with driving at 100 mph.

5. In the Bible, God sometimes told his people to do unusual things, and they did them without question:

- The prophet Ezekiel was told to lie on his left side for 390 days, then his right side for 40 days (Ezekiel. 4). This act dramatized his divided nation's sin and the reasons for their punishment. The 390 days represented the 390 years Israel had worshipped the golden calves; the 40 days, the number of years of the nation of Judah's sin and idolatry.
- God asked Ananias to seek out his enemy, the chief persecutor of Christians, Saul of Tarsus and pray with him (Acts 9.10–19). Ananias would risk his life by meeting Saul who had authority to arrest all believers, but Saul, who had been blinded, not only received his sight as Ananias prayed, but was also filled with the Holy Spirit and baptized.
- The prophet Isaiah walked stripped and barefoot through the streets of Jerusalem for three years at God's command (Isaiah 20). The prophet's shameful behaviour illustrated his own nation's shameful actions in putting their trust in foreign military alliances instead of in God.

6. Rules exist to make life easier for us, and even if they seem worthless or pointless we must remember they are there for a reason.

 Time for reflection

Lord,
Teach us the value of obeying the rules.
We cannot know the reasons behind everything,
So we put our trust in you,
who are all-knowing and all-wise;
through your holy name.
Amen.

Song

'He who would valiant be' (*Come and Praise*, 44)

REWARDS

By Stuart Kerner

Suitable for Whole School

 ### Aim

To reflect on the fact that the easy option isn't always the best. This assembly is particularly appropriate for groups who are close to exams.

 ### Preparation and materials

- Some enticing chocolate (e.g. a Ferrero Rocher).
- A lump of Blu Tak with a pound coin hidden inside (lying on the floor and looking much trodden on).
- A chewed and battered pen with a five pound note secreted inside the barrel (left seemingly discarded on the floor nearby).
- Bible reading: Luke 15.11–24.

 ### Assembly

1. Begin by asking for a volunteer. Say that you are feeling generous today and give the volunteer the chocolate. Ask whether they would like to eat it now or wait until you've finished speaking and swap it for something else that might be better. Hopefully they will agree to wait. (Just in case they choose to eat it, have some more chocolate on hand for another, more patient, volunteer!)
2. Say to your audience that they may know a story Jesus told, which is often referred to as 'The Prodigal Son' – ask if anyone knows what the word 'prodigal' means. The word means 'wasteful and extravagant' like the young man in this story. Read Luke 15.11–24.

3. Tell the audience that sometimes quick fixes and easy options that we think will get us what we want, usually lead us into disappointment and regret.

4. Going out with your mates when you should be revising for exams may seem like a great idea at the time – revision can be very dull and boring – but when you fail to get the qualifications you need, regret is all you will have left.

5. Now tell your volunteer that they have been very patient and you are now in a position to offer them something else instead of the chocolate.

6. Look flustered as though you have lost your swap items, and hurriedly pick up the Blu Tak and pen from the floor. With an unconvincing smile offer these to your volunteer as an exchange for the chocolate. The chances are they will be refused.

7. Show the audience the Blu Tak and pen saying that these seem like far less attractive options than the chocolate, but ... (pull the Blu Tak apart revealing the pound coin and remove the £5 note from the pen) ... perhaps the seemingly less attractive option is sometimes the better one!

 Time for reflection

If life were an event in the Olympics, it would be an endurance trial like the decathlon, not a sprint like the 100 metres.

The grass is sometimes greener, but only because the other field probably contains more cowpats!

Lord,
Grant us a vision of what you would have us do with our lives,
and give us the confidence to keep going when things get tough.
Help us to avoid taking the easy option,
and supply us with patience and endurance to complete the course.
Amen.

Song

'The Lord's my shepherd' (*Come and Praise*, 56)

THE TIME OF YOUR LIFE

By Helen Hinxman

Suitable for Key Stage Three

 Aim

To reflect on the fact that time is a precious commodity that requires wisdom in its use.

 Preparation and materials

- The computations for the school year could be accompanied by volunteers holding up large number cards and, to fit between them, three cards with minus, plus and equal signs. This will make a visual display of each new sum (see point 5).
- Bible readings: Psalm 90.1–10 and Ecclesiastes 3.1–8.

 Assembly

1. Say that before he wrote *The Lord of the Rings*, J. R. R. Tolkien wrote a book called *The Hobbit*. In this book, Gollum and Bilbo Baggins have a contest in which they ask each other riddles. This is life or death for Bilbo. Here's one of the riddles:

   This thing all things devours:
   Birds, beasts, trees, flowers;
   Gnaws iron, bites steel;
   Grinds hard stones to meal;
   Slays king, ruins town,
   And beats high mountain down.

2. The answer is, of course, time. Time is the most precious commodity we possess, but it moves on relentlessly and there's no way we can stop it, slow it down or reverse it. All we can do is measure it, waste it or use it wisely.

82

3. In the past, time was measured using sun, water, fire and sand: there were sundials, water clocks, candle clocks and hour glasses (egg timers). Then mechanical clocks were created: grandfather clocks, pocket watches, and wrist-watches. Today we have atomic clocks that are accurate to within microseconds.

4. Of course, regardless of how we measure it, time seems to go by quickly or slowly depending on what we are doing. If you're stuck in bed with chickenpox, time seems to drag. If you're at an amusement park, on the other hand, it flies by and before you know it, it's time to go home.

5. Say to the audience that they might think, for instance, that they spend ages at school, but that you will now demonstrate that they don't have time to come to school at all.

   - There are 365 days in a year. You have 13½ weeks holiday in a year, which is 95 days.
     ... 365 minus 95 leaves 270 days.
   - On average, you sleep for 9 hours each night; in one year this makes 3,285 hours, which is the same as 136 days.
     ... 270 minus 136 leaves 134 days.
   - You spend about 2 hours of every day eating. In one year this makes 730 hours, which is the same as 30 days.
     ... 134 minus 30 leaves 104 days.
   - But you don't come to school on Saturdays and Sundays and with 52 weeks in a year, that makes 104 days.
     ... 104 minus 104 leaves 0.

6. So in fact you don't seem to have time to come to school at all!

7. Conclude by saying that how we tell the time is very interesting but it is not as important as how we use our time. Do you use it thoughtlessly, and are irritable and grumpy when you can't have your own way? Or do you use your time thoughtfully, being happy and making the most of life?

8. Thank your audience for taking the time to listen.

 ## Time for reflection

Christians believe that God is eternal and exists outside the limitations of time. We do not, and so we must always be aware of the passage of time and how we behave within it. This famous passage from the Old Testament book of Ecclesiastes emphasizes this natural order. As you listen, think about whether or not you use your time wisely:

A time for everything

There is a time for everything,
and a season for every activity under heaven:
a time to be born and a time to die,
a time to plant and a time to uproot,
a time to kill and a time to heal,
a time to tear down and a time to build,
a time to weep and a time to laugh,
a time to mourn and a time to dance,
a time to scatter stones and a time to gather them,
a time to embrace and a time to refrain,
a time to search and a time to give up,
a time to keep and a time to throw away,
a time to tear and a time to mend,
a time to be silent and a time to speak,
a time to love and a time to hate,
a time for war and a time for peace.

Ecclesiastes 3.1–8

Eternal God,
Giver of time and opportunity,
make us successful stewards of these precious gifts,
and grant us the wisdom to handle them with care.
Amen.

 ### Song

'Time is a thing' (*Come and Praise*, 104)

MISSION IMPOSSIBLE

By Stuart Kerner

Suitable for Key Stage Three

Aim

To reflect on scepticism and encourage faith.

Preparation and materials

- Some volunteers to read out the examples of scepticism (see point 2).
- A copy of the readings for each reader.
- Bible readings: Matthew 17.14–20 and John 20.24–9.

Assembly

1. Ask if anyone knows what a sceptic is. Hopefully you will receive the correct answer, which is that sceptics are people who always say that things can't be done – doubters who are fond of saying, 'That's impossible.' You can find sceptics everywhere. You probably know people like this, or maybe you are the kind of person who pours scorn on the ideas of others and refuses to believe in schemes that seem fantastic.

2. Consider these examples of scepticism from the nineteenth century, which all suggested that things we now take for granted were impossible (ask your volunteers to read them out).

    - Joshua Coppersmith was arrested for trying to sell shares in a new invention called the telephone. Following his arrest, part of his police statement read: 'All well-informed people know that it is impossible to transmit the human voice over a wire.'

- In the nineteenth century scientists stated that the opening of the railways would require the construction of many new mental hospitals because people would be driven insane from horror at the sight of locomotives rushing across the country. Furthermore, they stated that if trains went as fast as 15 mph, blood would gush from the passengers' noses and they would suffocate when going through tunnels.
- In 1881, when the Young Women's Christian Association announced typing lessons for women, spirited objections were made on the grounds that the female body would break down under the strain.
- The first successful cast-iron plough was patented in 1797, but was rejected by many farmers on the grounds that cast iron poisoned the land and encouraged the growth of weeds.

3. Say: perhaps the sceptics among us should remember that sometimes doubts can lead to spectacularly wrong conclusions!
4. Christians read in the Bible that their faith keeps unbelief, scepticism and doubt away. After his resurrection, Jesus was confronted with the scepticism of one of his closest disciples. To the sceptic Thomas, Jesus said, 'Stop doubting and believe' (John 20.27). He also stated to his disciples, 'Nothing will be impossible for you' (Matthew 17.20).
5. So look ahead! Take a chance! Forget the doubters and dream your dreams. And when someone says it can't be done, conclude that with God's help it can!

 Time for reflection

Keep Doubt Out!

When you think your idea's mad,
When they tell you, 'You're so sad!',
When the world laughs at your vision,
Remember that you're on a mission.
Keep Doubt Out!

Keep your hopes and spirits high.
Forget the sceptics with their lies.
Build your castles in the air.
Never give in to despair.
Keep Doubt Out!
Stuart Kerner

Lord,
Through our faith in you,
help us to persevere against doubt,
make us strong enough to resist scorn,
grant us triumph over adversity.
Amen.

 Song

'My faith, it is an oaken staff' (*Come and Praise*, 46)

THE SECRETS OF SUCCESS

By Joanne Sincock

Suitable for Key Stage Three

Aim

To consider how we succeed in life.

Preparation and materials

- You might like to transfer each of the five secrets on to an OHP transparency or PowerPoint list.

Assembly

1. Have you ever heard people talk of 'the secrets of success'? All too often they are trying to sell you these 'secrets' for a very high price!
2. Go to any bookshop and you will find shelves of books offering you the keys to success. Many TV shows claim to give you all the tips you need to be an overnight success. Look up 'the secrets of success' on an internet search engine and you will receive over 12 million hits.
3. Today I am going to give you five secrets of success, and I'm not even going to charge you for this valuable information!
4. *'Secret' No 1 – People* Dealing with other people can be difficult, but we all know we should be well-mannered and polite. You need to accept the fact that you cannot please everybody. When you come across someone you cannot please, no matter what you do, just deal with that person firmly, but respectfully and politely. Quite simply, the secret is to treat people as you would like to be treated!
5. *'Secret' No 2 – Hard Work* Despite what many people have said, it's not easy to get rich overnight or to pass all your exams without revising – it just doesn't happen. To be

successful you will need to work, and work hard. Thomas Edison, the most successful inventor of all time, once said, 'There is no substitute for hard work.'

6. *'Secret' No 3 – Commitment* Expanding on the hard work 'secret', you will need to make a commitment to success. You must be willing to make sacrifices and work long hours. This will not happen overnight – it could take years. Are you prepared for years of frustration, hard work, ups and downs, dealing with people (good and bad), rejections and everything else that comes along with success?

7. *'Secret' No 4 – Pride* Take pride in your work. Your work will be a reflection of you. For success, build up a reputation for solid, good work. Be true to yourself and your work.

8. *'Secret' No 5 – Goals* Be aware of what you want and how you want to get it. Don't go ahead blindly without some planning of your goals and accomplishments. Use short-term, smaller goals to reach your long-term, ultimate goal. This will keep any fear of failure at bay too.

9. Of course, these so-called 'secrets' are mostly common sense. We all know these 'secrets'. We just have to apply them and use them consistently.

 ## Time for reflection

You've failed many times. Although you may not remember, you fell down the first time you tried to walk. You almost drowned the first time you tried to swim, didn't you? Did you hit the ball the first time you swung a bat or racquet? R. H. Macy failed seven times before his store in New York caught on. Novelist John Creasey got 753 rejection slips before he published 564 books. Don't worry about failure. Worry about the chances you miss when you don't even try.

To be a star, you must shine your own light, follow your own path, and not worry about the darkness, for that is when stars shine brightest.

> May the road rise to meet you;
> may the wind always be at your back;
> may the sun shine warm upon your face;
> may the rain fall softly upon your fields.

And until we meet again,
may God hold you in the palm of his hand.
Amen.

An old Celtic prayer

'He who would valiant be' (*Come and Praise*, 44)

TELEVISION

By Stuart Kerner

Suitable for Key Stage Three

Aim

To reflect on the detrimental effects of too much television.

Preparation and materials

- Transfer the 'Interesting facts about TV' on to an OHP transparency or a PowerPoint display.
- You might like to challenge some interested students to put the case for TV.

Assembly

1. Pose the following question: If you came home and found a strange man teaching your younger brothers or sisters to punch each other and to swear, or trying to sell them all kinds of stuff that they didn't need or was harmful to them, what would you do? (Take suggestions.) The chances are you would probably ask them to leave, or even throw them out.
2. Have you ever thought that this is exactly what television does? Yet in many houses it is often on from morning until night.
3. Today, watching television often means fighting, violence and foul language – and that's just deciding who gets to hold the remote control!
4. People who run television companies say that images of violence on TV do not have any lasting influence on the minds of viewers, but have you considered that the same people are perfectly willing to sell advertising time in order to do just that?

5. Ask: How many hours each day do you think people spend watching the television. After some contributions, display the following 'Interesting Facts about TV'.

Interesting Facts about TV

- Number of 30-second adverts seen in a year by an average child: 20,000.
- Number of minutes per week that parents spend in meaningful conversation with their children: 38.5.
- Number of minutes per week that the average child watches television: 1,680.
- Percentage of children aged 6 to 17 who have televisions in their bedrooms: 50.
- Hours per year the average young person spends in school: 900.
- Hours per year the average young person watches television: 1,500.

6. Comment that someone once described television as 'chewing gum for the eyes'. Just as many people chew constantly, so others seem to spend all their free time looking at the box, letting it drain their imaginations, tell them what to think and buy, and waste their lives.

7. Observe that there is a usually a button on the television to turn up the brightness, but watching television for hours on end has the opposite effect on the brains of many people! However, a famous comedian once remarked, 'I find television to be very educating. Every time somebody turns on the set, I go in the other room and read a book!'

8. Suggest that life has more to offer than just watching other people on the 'goggle box'. Through reading, taking part in church and community work, by getting involved in sports and hobbies – or even by having conversations with our families – our lives will be richer and far more interesting.

9. TV can destroy our imagination and make us very dull people indeed. Finally, by way of illustration, say that when television returned to Britain after the Second World War, a survey was done asking children whether they preferred television or radio – and why. One seven-year-old boy said he preferred radio 'because the pictures are better'.

Time for reflection

The 23rd Channel

The TV is my shepherd, I shall not want.
It makes me lie down on the sofa.
It leads me away from the faith.
It destroys my soul.
It leads me in the path of sex and violence for the sponsor's
sake.
Yea, though I walk in the shadow of Christian responsi-
bilities,
There will be no interruption, for the TV is with me.
Its cable and remote control, they comfort me.
It prepares an advertisement for me in the presence of my
worldliness.
It anoints my head with humanism and consumerism.
My coveting runneth over.
Surely, laziness and ignorance shall follow me all the days of
my life,
And I shall dwell in the house watching TV for ever.

Author unknown

 Song

'I belong to a family' (*Come and Praise*, 69)

COMMON SENSE

By Stuart Kerner

Suitable for Key Stage Three

Aim

To reflect on the need for common sense.

Preparation and materials

- You could prepare volunteers to read the insurance reports (see point 4).

Assembly

1. Ask your audience if they can say which senses are needed to drive a car. Hopefully, they should say: sight, hearing and touch.
2. Say that for most people there is also a sixth sense that is required, and ask if anyone can guess what it is. You may get some strange answers related to seeing dead people, etc. but you may get the answer you require, which is, of course, common sense.
3. Comment that this is sometimes sadly lacking and many people on the roads seem to use no sense at all.
4. Say that when people have an accident in their cars, they have to fill in a form or write a report of what happened for the insurance company. Tell them you have some examples of genuine reports that you would like to share, all of which demonstrate that common sense is often lacking (use as many or as few as you feel appropriate).

    - 'I started to slow down but the traffic was more stationary than I thought.'

- 'I pulled into a lay-by with smoke coming from under the bonnet. I realized the car was on fire so took my dog and smothered it with a blanket.'
- Q: Could either driver have done anything to avoid the accident?
  A: Travelled by bus?
- 'I didn't think the speed limit applied after midnight.'
- 'Windscreen broken. Cause unknown. Probably Voodoo.'
- 'The car in front hit the pedestrian but he got up so I hit him again.'
- 'I had been driving for 40 years when I fell asleep at the wheel and had an accident.'
- 'I pulled away from the side of the road, glanced at my mother-in-law and headed over the embankment.'
- 'Coming home, I drove into the wrong house and collided with a tree I don't have.'
- 'I thought my window was down, but I found out it wasn't when I put my head through it.'
- 'A pedestrian hit me and went under my car.'
- 'The guy was all over the road. I had to swerve a number of times before I hit him.'
- 'I had been shopping for plants all day and was on my way home. As I reached an intersection a hedge sprang up obscuring my vision and I did not see the other car.'
- 'To avoid hitting the bumper of the car in front I struck the pedestrian.'
- 'An invisible car came out of nowhere, struck my car and vanished.'
- 'I am sure the old fellow would never make it to the other side of the road when I ran him over.'
- 'The pedestrian had no idea which way to run, so I ran over him.'
- 'I saw a slow-moving, sad faced old gentleman, as he bounced off the roof of my car.'

5. Make the point that even the best of us have moments when our brains seem to disappear, and that although these statements are funny, there's a serious point behind them.
6. The sense we must always develop above all others is common sense.

Time for reflection

The Lord he gave us senses – five –
To help us through, and stay alive.
Our eyes can light the path ahead,
Our ears tell us what has been said,
Our hands can touch and feel the way,
Our noses smell a fresh bouquet.
Our taste is vital when we feed,
But there's one more sense we really need.
This sense is not so scarce or rare.
It's not something beyond compare.
It's not so great, vast or immense,
It's nothing more than common sense.

Stuart Kerner

Almighty God,
Give us wisdom to avoid thoughtlessness,
and help us to exercise the common sense you have given us.
Through your loving guidance
make us responsive to the needs of others
and sensitive to our surroundings.
Amen.

 Song

''Tis the gift to be simple' (*Come and Praise*, 97)

THE BUTTERFLY EFFECT

By Stuart Kerner

Suitable for Key Stage Three

Aim

To consider how even the smallest of us can have a big effect on the world around us.

Preparation and materials

- You might like to buy some 'Magic Flyer' butterflies from your local greetings card shop. Before the assembly, wind them up and place them inside a notebook. When you open the book and genuine looking butterflies magically fly out, the effect is very impressive.

Assembly

1. Begin by saying you are thinking of a powerful creature that can cause untold harm and destruction to many. Ask your audience if they can guess which member of the animal kingdom you are thinking of. The chances are they will respond with 'a lion', 'a shark' or some similar man-eating animal.
2. If you have the 'Magic Flyer' butterflies primed, open your notebook now to release them, saying that perhaps this will give the audience a clue about which creature you're thinking of. Hopefully someone will now suggest a butterfly.
3. Comment that to say that such a beautiful and delicate thing as a butterfly could bring death and destruction sounds absurd but, according to a scientific theory called the 'butterfly effect', that is exactly what, potentially, it can do.
4. According to this theory a butterfly's wings create tiny changes in the atmosphere that each cause further changes,

and so on, until ultimately a tornado might appear or, for that matter, be prevented from appearing. So a butterfly flapping its wings in London could, through a chain of events, produce a tidal wave in Japan, thus destroying countless homes and their occupants.

5. Perhaps we have similar power to change events in our own lives, the lives of others and even the world. No matter how small and insignificant we are – or think we are – we can, if we put our minds to it, bring about amazing changes.

6. Ask your audience to listen to this story:

Once upon a time in a country far away, there was a great famine. People carefully hoarded whatever food they could find, hiding it even from their friends and neighbours.

One day a merchant drove his wagon into the village, sold a few of his goods and began asking questions as if he planned to stay for the night.

'There's nothing to eat in the whole region,' he was told. 'You'd best keep moving on.'

'Oh, I have everything I need,' he said. 'In fact, I was thinking of making some stone soup to share with all of you.' He pulled a great iron cooking pot from his wagon, filled it with water, and built a fire under it. Then, with great ceremony, he pulled an ordinary looking stone from a velvet bag and dropped it into the water.

By now, hearing a rumour of free food, most of the villagers had come to the square or watched from their windows. As the merchant sniffed the 'soup' and licked his lips in expectation, hunger began to overcome their disbelief.

'Ahhh,' the merchant said to himself quite loudly. 'I do like a tasty stone soup. Of course, stone soup with carrots, that's hard to beat.'

A villager approached hesitantly, looked around, and pulled a few small carrots from under his coat. When he surreptitiously added it to the pot, the merchant grinned. 'Splendid,' he cried, 'you know, I once had stone soup with carrots and a little scrap of chicken, and it was fit for a king.'

Then it was the village butcher who approached. He had a little piece of chicken under his apron. And so it went on – some potatoes, some onions, some cabbage, some mushrooms – until there finally was, indeed, a delicious meal for all to enjoy.

The villagers offered the merchant a great deal of money for the magic stone, but he refused to sell and travelled on the next day.

And from that time on, long after the famine had ended, the villagers reminisced about the finest soup they'd ever had. And one or two understood that the magic was in the sharing – and they began to share what they had.

7. The merchant in that story managed to change people's attitudes and so change their lives by using a small but effective trick. It was the butterfly effect. What effect can you have on other people today?

 Time for reflection

Somewhere in this world, someone holds the key to all of humanity's problems.

It could well be someone here today.

The future is in our hands.

With your help, we can create a more positive planet.

What can you do today, tomorrow, next week, next month, next year?

And if you think you simply haven't got enough time, energy, or resources, remember the story of the stone soup.

When we all give a little, we can achieve anything.

 Song

'One more step' (*Come and Praise*, 47)

Awe and Wonder

A SMALL BLUE DOT

By *Charlotte Benstead*

Suitable for Key Stage Three

 Aim

To encourage students to look at the universe around them with awe and wonder.

 Preparation and materials

- OHT of the picture of Earth taken from the Voyager probe. This can be downloaded from these websites:
  http://visibleearth.nasa.gov/cgi-bin/view_rec.php?vev1id=1947
  http://en.wikipedia.org/wiki/Pale_Blue_Dot
- A copy of *The Hitchhiker's Guide to the Galaxy* by Douglas Adams.
- Music: any science fiction film or series theme tune.

 Assembly

1. Greet the audience with a salutation from a science fiction film or TV series (e.g. 'May the force be with you' from *Star Wars*; 'Live long and prosper' from *Star Trek*, etc.). Ask if any of the audience have ever noticed how important we humans are always shown to be in any film or TV series. You might like to ask for some examples.

2. Show a copy of *The Hitchhiker's Guide to the Galaxy*. Writer Douglas Adams centres his story on an Earthman, Arthur Dent, one of a handful of survivors who remain when the planet is demolished to make way for a hyperspace by-pass. The tale is a despair-ridden one. Our world is 'an utterly insignificant blue/green planet', orbiting a 'small, unregarded sun at the unfashionable end of the Western spiral arm of the galaxy'. Indeed, the entire *Hitchhiker's*

Guide entry for 'Earth' reads nothing more than 'Mostly Harmless'.

3. A similar apparently depressing view of the place we call home was put forward by Carl Sagan (1934–96), who was born in New York, and from a humble background became a scientist, scholar and communicator. (You might like to add that Professor Sagan received 22 honorary degrees from American colleges and universities for his contributions to science, literature, education and the preservation of the environment, and many awards for his work on the long-term consequences of nuclear war and the need to reverse the nuclear arms race. Asteroid 2709 Sagan is named after him.)

4. When contemplating a photo of Earth taken from the Voyager spacecraft in deep interplanetary space, Carl Sagan said:

If you look at it, you see a dot.

That's here – that's home.

That's us. On it, everyone you ever heard of, every human being who ever lived, lived out their lives.

The aggregate of all our joys and sufferings, thousands of confident religions, ideologies and economic doctrines, every hunter and forager, every hero and coward, every creator and destroyer of civilizations, every king and peasant, every young couple in love, every hopeful child, every mother and father, every inventor and explorer, every teacher of morals, every corrupt politician, every superstar, every supreme leader, every saint and sinner in the history of our species – lived there on a mote of dust, suspended in a sunbeam.

The earth is a very small stage in a vast cosmic arena.

Think of the rivers of blood spilled by all those generals and emperors so that in glory and in triumph they could become the momentary masters of a fraction of a dot.

Think of the endless cruelties visited by the inhabitants of one corner of the dot on scarcely distinguishable inhabitants of some other corner of the dot.

How frequent their misunderstandings, how eager they are to kill one another, how fervent their hatreds.

Our posturings, our imagined self-importance, the delusion that we have some privileged position in the universe, are challenged by this point of pale light.

Our planet is a lonely speck in the great enveloping cosmic dark. In our obscurity – in all this vastness – there is no hint that help will come from elsewhere to save us from ourselves.

It is up to us.

Carl Sagan

5. Ask your audience to consider that there is perhaps no better demonstration of the folly of human vanity than this distant image of our tiny world. It emphasizes our responsibility to deal more kindly and compassionately with one another and to preserve and cherish that pale blue dot, the only home we've ever known.

6. For Christians and other religious believers the earth is more than just a small, pale blue dot – it is the creation of God: a mysterious, wonderful, sacred space.

 Time for reflection

Ask students to close their eyes and consider the relative smallness of an ant in comparison to a human being. Now ask them to consider the scene from the ant's point of view.

Alternatively, read this quote from Albert Einstein, and take a moment to reflect on it:

The most beautiful thing we can experience is the mysterious. It is the source of all true art and all science. He to whom this emotion is a stranger, who can no longer pause to wonder and stand rapt in awe, is as good as dead: his eyes are closed.

Albert Einstein

Lord,
We sometimes feel small and insignificant.
Help us to get our importance in perspective,
and allow us to realize that though small,
this seemingly insignificant small blue dot we inhabit
is your precious creation

and our precious home.
Amen.

 Hymn

'All things bright and beautiful' (*Come and Praise*, 3)

THE PROBLEM OF SIZE

By Stuart Kerner

Suitable for Key Stage Three

Aim

To understand that spiritual and emotional growth and not physical size are the most important things in life.

Preparation and materials

- The parable of the mustard seed can be found in Mark 4.30–32.

Assembly

1. Tell your audience that you are going to talk about an issue that may concern them, especially if they are still in Year Seven. This is the problem of size.
2. The writer of Psalm 8 in the Old Testament could see clearly when he said to God:

   I look up at your heavens, made by your fingers, at the moon and stars you set in place -- ah, what is man that you should spare a thought for him, the son of man that you should care for him?

   Psalm 8.3–4

3. The psalmist is saying: 'Look, God, I'm so small compared to the rest of your creation that I just don't see how I can be of any importance to you or anyone else.' Most of us have probably had thoughts like this from time to time.
4. Have you ever stood in the countryside late at night, and looked up at the sky, and been amazed at the stars you can see? The sky seems covered with stars.
5. And beneath such an amazing starlit sky, we might find ourselves asking the very same question as the writer of

Psalm 8. When the universe is so big and this earth, by comparison, is so small, and I am just one individual among so many millions of others, how can I possibly be of any importance to anyone, least of all to the Creator who made everything in heaven and on earth?

6. Obviously it is not easy to answer such a big question: perhaps we should concentrate on the scale of things.

7. First, you and I don't really attach all that much importance to size.

8. If we did, it would mean, for example, that we thought an elephant was more important than a horse and a lorry more important than a car, and that all of them were more important than a person.

9. But let's take it a stage further. If we really believed that 'size means importance', then someone weighing 15 stone and standing 6 feet tall would be much more important than someone who weighs 10 stone and is five feet tall. And by the same token, most children would matter less than most adults, and babies least of all. The fact is, of course, that we treat babies and young people as being in some respects more important than adults, particularly if they are part of our own family.

10. Jesus looks at this idea in the parable of the mustard seed and develops it a bit further. The mustard seed is a tiny seed yet it grows into the biggest shrub. Not over night, he reminds his hearers; it all takes time and the growth is largely unnoticed. Night and day, while people are sleeping or getting on with their lives, its growth continues according to God's plan. And all this growth is not just good for the seed, but also for the creatures that will turn to the bush for shelter when it has grown to fruition. The birds benefit as well.

11. So God's choosing you and me and the growth he has planned for us are not just for our sakes. He wants other people to depend upon us. Maybe he wants to give us children of our own. He certainly wants to use us as branches on which other people can depend and be supported.

12. So size doesn't matter. But growth (in the right direction) matters a great deal.

Time for reflection

When I was little

When I was little,
My mum said: 'You know,
I'll measure you weekly,
And see how you grow.'

So each week she measured
And then she would write
A mark on the door post
To dwell on my height.

Now I'm six foot
And can reach for the sky,
My mum seems much shorter
Which makes me ask why ...

Does height really matter?
When I think we all know
It's not the size of your body
But how much *you* grow.

For inside we never stop
Growing, you see,
It's what's big in my heart
That makes me *me*.

Stuart Kerner

 Song

'How great thou art' (*Mission Praise*, 173)

WHAT ARE YOU WORTH?

By Helen Hinxman

Suitable for Whole School

 Aim

To reflect on the value of each individual person.

 Preparation and materials

- Some test-tubes or jars which should contain real or pretend chemical powders and liquids.
- A bar of soap, a nail, a cup of sugar, a tin of whitewash, a box of matches, a salt cellar, and some flea powder.
- All of these should be placed on a table at the front and covered up until needed.
- A photo of a private jet (e.g. <www.airroyale.com/>).
- A photo of a semi-detached house (e.g. <www.koe-at.com/semideta.jpg>).
- A photo of a family car (e.g. <www.tuning.kvalitne.cz/Ford%20Focus%20stribrny.jpg>).
- A photo of a human being (e.g. <www.lz95.org/lzhs/social_studies/reimann/Vitruvian%20Man.jpg>).
- These could all be put on to OHP slides, or a PowerPoint display).
- Some A4 card and marker pens.

 Assembly

1. Ask for four volunteers to come to the front. Give each an A4 card and a marker pen. Say that you are going to show them four items and they should write down on the card how much money they think each one is worth.
2. Show the picture of the private jet. Give the volunteers time to think and write down their guesses about its value, then

reveal the true price of around £450,000. Repeat with the house (worth about £250,000), the car (£15,000) and the human body (£2.40). Ask someone to keep score and award a prize to the winner.

3. Ask if anyone was surprised that the human body wasn't worth more than the other three things. Explain that scientists have spent huge amounts of human and financial resources studying the composition, and calculating the worth, or worthlessness, of the human body. If we total the monetary value of the elements in our bodies and the average person's skin, we arrive at a sum of £2.40! Point out that this value is, however, subject to change, due to stock market fluctuations.

4. The elements in the human body break down as follows:

- 65 per cent oxygen
- 18.5 per cent carbon
- 9.5 per cent hydrogen
- 2 per cent nitrogen
- 1.5 per cent calcium
- 1 per cent phosphorus
- 0.4 per cent potassium

- 0.3 per cent sulphur
- 0.2 per cent sodium
- 0.2 per cent chlorine
- 0.1 per cent magnesium
- 0.1 per cent iron
- 0.1 per cent iodine

- Additionally, our bodies contain trace quantities of fluorine, silicon, manganese, zinc, copper, aluminium, and arsenic.

5. Reveal the various ingredients on your table. Say that in the non-scientist's terms, the human body also contains the following (refer to each prop as appropriate):

- Fat enough for seven bars of soap
- Iron enough for one medium-sized nail
- Sugar enough for 7 cups of tea
- Lime enough to whitewash a fence
- Phosphorus enough to tip 2,200 matches
- Magnesium enough for one dose of salts
- Potash enough to explode one toy crane
- Sulphur enough to rid one dog of fleas.

Together, all the above amounts to less than 50p!

6. Our most valuable asset is our skin, which Japanese scientists have studied extensively. They have discovered that the average person is the proud owner of 1.3 to 1.6 metres of skin, the variation depending on height and weight. Basing the skin's value on the selling price of cowhide, which is approximately £1.30 per square metre, the value of an average person's skin is about £1.87!

7. Unfortunately, all this makes us sound cheap and worthless, but we shouldn't be too downhearted. Christians believe that God made each of us in his image. In Psalm 139.14, the psalmist says, 'I praise you, for I am fearfully and wonderfully made.' And, more importantly, he loves each of us. So the psalmist says, 'The steadfast love of the LORD is from everlasting to everlasting on those who fear him' (Psalm 103.17).

We have limitless potential and the ability to shape our destiny – and that's something you can't put a price on!

 ## Time for reflection

This is what Martin Luther King, the great civil rights leader, said about the value of human beings:

> I guess, since the standards of living are a little higher today, you could get about a dollar ninety-eight for the average man. This is interesting. Think about it. Man's bodily stuff is worth only ninety-eight cents. But can we explain the whole of man in terms of ninety-eight cents? Can we explain the artistic genius of a Michelangelo in terms of ninety-eight cents? Can we explain the poetic genius of a Shakespeare in terms of ninety-eight cents? Can we explain the spiritual genius of Jesus of Nazareth in terms of ninety-eight cents? Can we explain the mystery of the human soul in terms of ninety-eight cents? Oh, no. There is something within man that cannot be explained in terms of dollars and cents. There is something within man that cannot be reduced to chemical and biological terms, for man is more than a tiny vagary of whirling electrons.

He is more than a wisp of smoke from a limitless smouldering. Man is a child of God.

Martin Luther King

Dear Lord,
Although we sometimes feel worthless and useless,
keep us ever mindful of the wonderful fact
that we are your creation.
Even if our bodies are inexpensive,
help us to remember that our souls are beyond price.
Amen.

 Song

'I am weak, but thou art strong' (*Mission Praise*, 263)

Christian Ideas

THE BIBLE

By Gill Hartley

Suitable for Key Stage 3

Aim

To explore and appreciate the variety in and inspiration of the Bible.

Preparation and materials

- A Bible, preferably a good modern translation, carried in a pocket/handbag/briefcase/shopping bag, etc.
- Organize the pupils from two classes to bring in one book each (on any subject) and bring in some spares yourself, to make up a total of 66 books.

Assembly

1. Ask the pupils to bring out the books they have brought in and to pile them up one by one. Suggest that the rest of the school counts the books out loud as they are piled up. You could read out and comment positively on some of the titles but try to avoid this section going on too long.
2. When you have counted up to the total of 66, ask the students if they would like to carry all those books at once? Tell them that you have 66 books in your pocket/handbag/briefcase/shopping bag! Bring out the Bible and explain that it is not just one book, but 66.
3. Ask if they know any of the titles of the individual books of the Bible. Among the answers may be:

   - Matthew, Mark, Luke, John (the Gospels);
   - Psalms;
   - Genesis.

Use any answers you receive to demonstrate the different sorts of books in the Bible, for example:

- Matthew, Mark, Luke, John – stories about Jesus' life (i.e. biography);
- Psalms – a book of poetry or songs;
- Genesis – stories of God's people long ago (i.e. history, myths, legends).

4. You might also want to talk about other sorts of books in the Bible, such as:

- Proverbs – a book of wise sayings and mottoes;
- Acts of the Apostles – stories of the first followers of Jesus (i.e. history);
- the Epistles (e.g. Romans, Corinthians, Ephesians) – letters written to the first Christian churches.

5. Illustrate some of the different sorts of literature to be found in the Bible by reading some extracts from a good modern translation or children's Bible, such as:

- one of the stories of Jesus' birth (e.g. Matthew chapter 2);
- a poem or song (e.g. Psalm 23);
- the beginning of the story of Noah, from long ago (Genesis 6.9 onwards).

6. Briefly explore with the children the division of the Bible into two sections: the Old Testament, which describes the time before Jesus was born, and the New Testament, which tells the story of Jesus and what his followers did after he died.

7. Ask what this collection of books called the Bible is for. After considering whatever answers you receive, explain that the Bible as a whole is considered a special book by Christians. Many people believe that God inspired all its different authors to write it to teach them what God is like.

8. Explain that other religions also use the Bible – the Old Testament is the special book of the Jewish people, and Muslims find the stories of Jesus helpful.

Time for reflection

Think about what you like to read.
What's the best book you've ever read? Think about it now and
    ask yourself why you like it so much.
What do you know about the Bible?
If you want you can join in quietly with this prayer:

> Dear God,
> Thank you for books,
> for writing,
> for the knowledge and fun and beauty and magic of stories,
> of history, of information and of all types of writing.
> Thank you for the Bible with all its different parts.
> **Amen.**

Song

'The ink is black' (*Come and Praise*, 67)

THE BODY BEAUTIFUL

By Charlotte Benstead

Suitable for Whole School

Aim

To compare the human body with the body of Christ, that is, the Church.

Preparation and materials

- Ask some students to read the facts about the body (see point 2).
- Bible reading: 1 Corinthians 12.12–26.

Assembly

1. Begin by telling your audience that they are amazing, really amazing – well, their bodies are, anyway.
2. Ask your readers to read out the following facts:

   - The body is composed of 70 trillion cells. That's 70 million million cells! 80 per cent of your body is water.
   - You breathe enough air throughout your lifetime to fill 10 million balloons.
   - The heart pumps 5 litres of blood through the body at any one time. An average heart beats over 100,000 times a day.
   - There are about 62,000 miles of blood vessels in the body. Put end to end, they could wrap around the world 2.5 times.
   - You consume 30 tons of food throughout your life.
   - The body's bacteria could fill a soup can.
   - The average head has 100,000 hairs, each living for about 2 to 4 years.

- Under normal conditions, during strenuous exercise you can secrete 2 pints of sweat per hour.
- You secrete 17 gallons of tears throughout your lifetime.

3. Comment that the human body is a marvellous work of God's creation. Every time you raise a finger or take a step, an infinite number of cells and nerves interact to produce such seemingly simple movements.
4. In the New Testament St Paul likens the Church to the human body. Read 1 Corinthians 12.12–26.
5. Just as each of your individual cells contributes to the whole body, so each of you must play your part to ensure that each community you belong to (family, school, local neighbourhood) works in the best way possible. Without the cooperation and joint effort of our brains, bones and muscles, we cannot move – without your cooperation with your fellow humans the world would be similarly paralysed.

 Time for reflection

This reflection is based on a meditation by St Teresa of Avila:

Christ has no body now but yours,
no hands, no feet, on earth but yours.
Yours are the eyes through which he looks
compassion on this world.
Yours are the feet
with which he walks to do good.
Yours are the hands
with which he blesses all the world.
Yours are the hands,
yours are the feet,
yours are the eyes.
You are his body.
Christ has no body now on earth but yours.

Dear God,
Bless our hands, that we may touch what is good.
Bless our feet, that we may walk in your path.
Bless our eyes, that we may look with compassion.
Bless our ears, that we may heed those in need.

Bless our mouths, that we may speak words of comfort.
Make each of our bodies a vital element of the body of
    Christ.
Amen.

 Song

'Breathe on me' (*Mission Praise*, 25)

FATHER, FORGIVE

By Guy Donegan-Cross

Suitable for Whole School

 Aim

To explore forgiveness.

 Preparation and materials

- A picture of the burnt cross from Coventry Cathedral. Download from <http://upload.wikimedia.org/wikipedia/en/0/07/Coventry_Cathedral_burnt_cross.jpg>.

 Assembly

1. Show the picture. Explain that on 14 November 1940 Coventry was heavily bombed by the Germans. The town was devastated, as was the cathedral. But the following morning the decision was taken to rebuild the cathedral – not as a gesture of defiance, but as a sign of faith and hope for the future.
2. Shortly after the destruction, the cathedral stonemason, Jock Forbes, noticed that two of the charred medieval roof timbers had fallen in the shape of a cross. He set them up in the ruins where they were later placed on an altar of rubble with the moving words, 'Father Forgive' inscribed on the sanctuary wall.
3. Today the ruins are still standing next to the modern cathedral. The cross is a reminder of the importance of forgiveness. But why should human beings try to forgive each other – especially in times of war?

4. Tell this story:

There was a priest in the Philippines who carried the burden of a secret sin he had committed many years before. He had repented but still had no sense of God's forgiveness.

In the priest's church was a woman who claimed to have visions in which she spoke with Jesus and he with her. The priest, however, was sceptical. To test her, he said, 'The next time you speak with Jesus, I want you to ask him what sin your priest committed while he was in Bible college.'

The woman agreed.

A few days later the priest asked, 'Well, did Christ visit you in your dreams?'

'Yes, he did,' she replied.

'And did you ask him what sin I committed in Bible college?'

'Yes.'

'Well, what did he say?'

'He said, "I don't remember."'

5. Christians believe that God forgives through Jesus. In this forgiveness there is hope for you, for me and for this broken world.

Time for reflection

Spend a moment thinking about the wooden cross.
Is there anyone you need to forgive?
Is there anything for which you need to be forgiven?

Lord God,
Please forgive me.
Thank you that you do not hold things against me.
Teach me to be like you
so the world can be a better place.
Amen.

Song

'God is love' (*Come and Praise*, 36)

Inspiring people

LIFE IS LIKE A BOX OF CHOCOLATES – GEORGE CADBURY

by Caroline Edwards

Suitable for Key Stage Three

 Aim

To think about the fruits of putting our beliefs into practice.

 Preparation and materials

- You might like to stick the Harvard University research to a real newspaper for authenticity.
- A large bar of chocolate.
- A box of Cadbury's Miniature Heroes chocolates.
- A photo of George Cadbury. There is a photograph at <www.spartacus.schoolnet.co.uk/REcadbury.htm>.
- You can find out more about Quakerism at <www.quaker.org.uk/>.
- Bible reading: 'Taste and see that the Lord is good' (Psalm 34.8).
- Suggested music: 'Chocolate' by Kylie Minogue and 'Sweet like chocolate' by Shanks and Bigfoot.

 Assembly

1. Enter the assembly munching on a large and obvious chocolate bar – the bigger the better.
2. Appearing oblivious to the audience reaction, tell your audience that you recently read the following item in the newspaper:

   Researchers at Harvard University in America have carried out experiments that suggest that if you eat chocolate three times a month you will live almost a year longer than those who forgo such sweet temptation.

But it's not all good news – the Harvard research also suggested that people who eat too much chocolate have a lower life expectancy. Chocolate's high fat content means that excessive indulgence can contribute to obesity, leading to an increased risk of heart disease.

But if you can't resist chocolate, at least stick to dark chocolate. It's higher in cocoa than milk chocolate and helps to increase levels of HDL, a type of cholesterol that helps prevent fat clogging up arteries.

3. Comment that perhaps this should be a lesson to us, as it looks like the old adage of 'everything in moderation' still holds true.
4. Ask how many students have eaten more than three pieces of chocolate in the last month. A show of hands will probably indicate the majority. Ask how many have eaten three pieces in the last week and then how many in the last 24 hours. Comment that chocolate is clearly one of the most popular foods in the school – even if it can be harmful to our health.
5. Ask if anyone knows where the phrase 'life is like a box of chocolates' comes from. Of course, it was said by the actor Tom Hanks in his Oscar-award-winning portrayal of Forrest Gump, in the film of the same name.
6. Now produce your box of 'Miniature Heroes' and ask for the assistance of two volunteers who should join you at the front of the assembly.
7. Empty the box on to a table in front of the volunteers and tell them you are going to read them a story which contains the names of all the various chocolates in the box. Whenever they hear one of the names they should grab that particular chocolate and throw it into the audience. Whoever is the fastest gains a point, and the volunteer with the most points gets the remaining chocolates as a prize (you may want another member of staff to adjudicate).

Here is the passage to be read:

Last night I had a DREAM. I dreamt I was in a field of cows, having a PICNIC. I needed some TIME OUT as I'd been working so hard. The field was near the DAIRY. MILK was being sold there. I bought some, but as I passed the nearest cow its tail began to TWIRL, and a giant cowpat, the colour of CARAMEL, came hurtling out! As I trod in the CRUNCHIE dung, I quietly said to myself, 'Oh, FUDGE!' Then I woke up.

8. Once the pandemonium has died down thank your volunteers and present the winner with their booty.
9. Tell the audience that the man who founded Cadbury's was more than just a miniature hero. To the people he employed he was an enormous one! Now tell the story of George Cadbury.

About 150 years ago, factory owners had to build houses for the people who came from the villages to work in their factories. Many factory owners built very small houses, often back to back, which soon became slums. These factory owners were more concerned with making money than with the well-being of those who worked for them.

George Cadbury was different. He was born on 19 September 1839, the son of John Cadbury,

When George and his brother Richard took over the factory from their father, business was bad. The public wouldn't drink chocolate because it was too bitter! George heard that a Dutch chocolate manufacturer had invented a machine to press out the sweet cocoa butter. George said, 'I went off to Holland without knowing a word of Dutch, saw the manufacturer, with whom I had to talk entirely by signs and a dictionary, and bought the machine.'

So it was that in 1866 Cadbury's put on the market the first pure cocoa essence that tasted sweet. Business soon boomed. As well as drinking chocolate, tablets of chocolate were now manufactured.

But George Cadbury cared for more than business. He was a Christian, a member of the Society of Friends, also called Quakers. Every Sunday – his one day off – he set off at 6.30 a.m. to take Class 14 in the newly formed Adult School. He took a flower for each member of his class. He described this school as 'a sort of co-operative system of carrying on class where one is our Master, even Christ'. And in true Quaker style, all were treated as equals, though many were down-and-outs. All kinds of Christians joined in. Reading and writing came first on the programme and Bible study followed.

In the Cadbury factory, each day began with Bible reading and prayers for all. But no one could call the Cadbury brothers hypocrites. Their Christianity never stopped at fine words. In an age when most owners cared little about conditions for their workers, George believed in providing first-class facilities. When the premises became too small, he decided to build a factory in the country. The brothers bought a site a few miles out of Birmingham, which they called 'Bournville'.

George loved open spaces. He provided football fields, a playground and a garden with a lily pond. Inside, there were warm cloakrooms for drying off wet clothes and a warming cupboard for the workers to heat their own food.

But working out of town presented transport problems. George decided to buy land round the factory and build a village for his workforce. Every house would have a spacious garden big enough to grow vegetables. Fruit trees were planted and the garden dug over before each new owner moved in. Trees were planted along the wide roads. Later, George Cadbury built schools and a shopping area.

George Cadbury said: 'Why should an industrial area be squalid and depressing? Why should not the industrial worker enjoy country air without being separated from his work? If the country is a good place to live in, why not to work in?'

10. Now say that today Cadbury's has factories all over the world – Australia, New Zealand, Malaysia, India, Indonesia, Japan and several countries in Africa. Recent developments include new factories in China and Poland.

   Cadbury's chocolate is sold all over North America and in Europe. Many countries also receive their Cadbury's chocolates straight from Bournville, making it a worldwide success story.

11. Finish by saying we owe a lot to people such as these, who had good new ideas and whose sincere Christian beliefs

made them care enough for others to want to offer them the best conditions they could.

 ## Time for reflection

We thank you, Lord,
for the example of those who have learned about you,
and then showed their love for you by caring for others.
Help us to be more like them.
Amen.

 ## Song

'Fill thou my life' (*Come and Praise*, 41)

HOPE CAN MOVE MOUNTAINS – NORMAN CROUCHER

By Stuart Kerner

Suitable for Whole School

Aim

To help us realize that we should never give up hope, and that through faith we can overcome any obstacle.

Preparation and materials

- You might like to visit Norman Croucher's website:

Assembly

1. Ask the students what they hope will happen to them in the future. You might expect answers like good GCSE results, success, fame, money, children, happiness.
2. Now ask what obstacles might stand in their way. Answers will probably include health worries, lack of self-belief, low self-esteem, lack of the right qualifications.
3. Tell them that if they genuinely hope for these things, they must remember that hope is all about never giving up. It is about keeping your eyes firmly fixed on your goal and going for it, no matter what.
4. Ask your audience to imagine that above all else they liked climbing mountains. But then they had an accident and lost both their legs. What would they do? Feel sorry for themselves? Give up?
5. Here is a true story about a man who faced this very problem and refused to give up.

129

When he was young, Norman Croucher enjoyed rock-climbing in his home county of Cornwall. Then one night, when he was 19 years old, an awful accident happened that for many would have meant the end of an active life.

Norman fell down a railway bank on to the railway line and into the path of a train, which took both his legs off below the knee.

Norman refused to give in to this tragedy. He couldn't wait to learn how to use his new artificial limbs so that he could start climbing again. The process was difficult and painful. He began by climbing trees, and then moved on to climbing small mountains.

More determined than ever, Norman aimed higher. In 1969, in order to increase his strength to take on bigger mountains, he undertook a sponsored walk from John o' Groats to Land's End – the furthest distance it is possible to walk across the UK. He succeeded in walking the 874 miles in three months, raising for Oxfam more than £1,000, which in 1969 was a great deal of money.

The next year Norman began climbing in the Swiss Alps and two years later he successfully climbed the Eiger.

Norman was chosen as a 'Man of the Year' in 1971, and again in 1978, and in 1977 he received an OBE from the Queen for his voluntary work for disabled people. He was also the first disabled person to be appointed to the Sports Council.

Of course, Norman Croucher has conquered mountains of a different kind too. He had faith in himself and never gave up hope. Not only has he shown just what a differently abled person can do, but he has also given great encouragement and hope to many people who are faced with problems that seem impossible to overcome.

6. You might not be able to climb mountains, but if you keep your hopes up, you might be able to move them. As Jesus said, 'In the world you will have trouble, but be brave: I have conquered the world' (John 16.33).

Time for reflection

Hope looks for the good in people instead of harping on the
worst.

Hope opens doors where despair closes them.

Hope discovers what can be done instead of grumbling about
what cannot.

Hope 'lights a candle' instead of 'cursing the darkness'.

Hope regards problems, small or large, as opportunities.

Hope cherishes no illusions, nor does it yield to cynicism.

Hope sets big goals and is not frustrated by repeated difficulties
or setbacks.

Hope pushes ahead when it would be easy to quit.

Hope puts up with modest gains, realizing that 'the longest
journey starts with one step'.

Hope accepts misunderstandings as the price for serving the
greater good of others.

Hope is a good loser because it has the divine assurance of final
victory.

> Lord,
> when things seem to be going wrong,
> when we feel discouraged and tired,
> help us to put our faith in you.
> Give us the patience we need to trust in your loving care
> and give us the precious gift of hope.
> **Amen.**

 Song

'Tell out my soul' (*Mission Praise*, 631)

READ IT ALOUD – STEVE TURNER

By *Charlotte Benstead*

Suitable for Key Stage Three

Aim

To consider the talents of poets.

Preparation and materials

- Find a dull poem (see point 1).
- Readers for Steve Turner's poems (see point 5.)
- More information about Steve Turner can be found on <www.lion-publishing.co.uk/pages/data.asp?layout=page.htm&id=272>.
- Most of Steve Turner's poems can be found here: <www.poemhunter.com/steve-turner/poet-6839/> and <www.rejesus.co.uk/expressions/steve_turner/>.

Assembly

1. Ask anyone who likes reading poetry to raise their hand. Whatever response you get, enthusiastically say that you would like to read them some poetry. Start reading the dullest, most boring poem you can find. (The works of William Topaz McGonagall are widely believed to be some of the worst poetry ever committed to paper, many can be found at <http://www.dundee22.freeserve.co.uk/default.htm>.) Read until you see your audience's eyes begin to glaze over, and admit that some poetry can be quite dull.
2. Continue by saying that for Steve Turner poetry at school had been boring. A common means of punishment at his school had been to make students write out a poem – a long one – for detention. Then there was poetry-learning. What the poem meant didn't seem to matter – it was the

132

memorizing that was important. Enough to kill any poem stone dead, as it had for Steve Turner by the time he left school with two GCSEs to start work in a clothing factory.

3. In the 1960s he came across the lyrics to the songs of the Beatles and Bob Dylan, and later he began writing poetry himself. The big change came when he heard poetry read out at a nearby pub. Despite feeling very nervous, Steve plucked up the courage to read out some of his own poems. After that, Steve Turner the poet really took off.

4. Steve now reads his poems in churches, prisons, schools, art centres and at festivals, as well as in pubs. He believes it's the sound of the poems as they are read out loud that makes people keen to read and think about poems for themselves.

5. At this point read a couple of Steve's poems (you could rehearse a couple of readers in advance). Two of the poems most suitable are: 'Heaven' and 'Christmas is really for the children'.

6. Poets are people who observe what the rest of us don't notice. Steve Turner sees our world sharply and clearly and, because he is a Christian, he sees it with the insights that his faith brings. What he has to say makes people sit up. He doesn't aim to be popular, and the off-beat humour of his poems doesn't disguise their bite. Steve Turner's poetry gets under our skin even while it's making us smile.

 Time for reflection

> O God,
> who created the earth through the power of your word,
> we thank you for the talent of poets like Steve Turner.
> You have given us the power of speech
> and the ability to make words both beautiful and thought-
>   provoking.
> Allow us to see the world with a poet's eye,
> and appreciate it with a poet's heart.
> **Amen.**

 Song

'How sweet the name of Jesus sounds' (*Mission Praise*, 78)

WHAT HATH GOD WROUGHT!

by Stuart Yeates

Suitable for Whole School

Aim

To consider the importance of perseverance and the value of communication.

Preparation and materials

- You might like to practise the Morse code.
- Bible reading: Numbers 23.23.

Assembly

1. Imagine a world without telephones, television, email or the internet, where the only way to communicate with people over a long distance would be either to write a letter or send a carrier pigeon!
2. In 1830, it took five to eight months for a letter from the UK to reach India! Imagine that – by the time you found out something had happened it would be just a distant memory to those involved. By 1879 a telegram could arrive in Bombay in five hours, a definite improvement.
3. The invention that made this possible was the telegraph, invented in 1844 by Samuel Morse. Morse also invented a special code made up of dots and dashes, which could be sent along the telegraph wire and decoded at the other end.
4. For instance: (tap out the following Morse Code: .... . .-.. .-.. – – –). That means 'Hello'.
5. Samuel Morse, the son of a Christian minister, loved to study the Bible. He started one of the first Sunday Schools in America and served as its supervisor.

6. In 1818, at the age of 27, he married a girl called Lucretia. Seven years later Morse went to Washington DC to work as a painter. However, owing to the lack of quick communication, Lucretia had died and was buried before Samuel had even received a letter informing him she was ill. This tragedy spurred Samuel on to find a fast way to transmit news.

7. Before completing his invention, Morse suffered many setbacks. For instance, at his first public demonstration of the telegraph, in 1842, he laid a wire across a New York harbour, but before he could complete his transmission, a ship's anchor caught the line and cut it.

8. Finally, in 1844, he strung together a series of overhead lines between Washington DC and Baltimore, and transmitted the first public telegraph message: 'What hath God wrought!' This was a phrase taken from the book of Numbers in the Bible. Morse said that his invention of the telegraph was 'God's work, and he alone carried me this far through all my trials and enabled me to triumph over obstacles, physical and moral, which opposed me.'

9. The first telegraph message sent sounded like this (tap it out):

```
.-- .... .- -/
.... .- - ..../
--. --- -../
.-- .-. --- ..- --. .... - ..--..
```

10. People at the time responded in various ways to Morse's exclamation, 'What hath God wrought [done]!' Some were confident that the telegraph was a gift of God for building up community and worldwide communication; others were fearful and cynical.

11. However, while some were confident and some fearful, a forward-seeing few were aware of the potential of the new technology.

12. Through people like Samuel Morse, whose faith was never shaken and who always persevered, we are now able to enjoy almost unlimited communication and access to information. There are examples of parents finding medical solutions unknown to their home doctors. People can also get in touch in emergencies, find long-lost friends

and members of their family, and educate others living in remote areas of the world.

13. These days mobile phones and the internet also arouse mixed reactions, with the difference that today people seldom refer to God. For Christians, of course, communication is central. In the beginning was the Word, God's communication with us.

 ## Time for reflection

Lord God,
You created everything through your Word.
Help us to use the technology we have
to communicate with others:
to comfort the lonely,
give hope to the desperate,
and spread your love throughout the world.
Amen.

 ## Song

'It's a new day' (*Come and Praise*, 106)

Assemblets

WHO'S PACKING YOUR PARACHUTE?

During the Second World War, Group Captain Giles Gantry took part in more than 50 missions over enemy territory in his Lancaster bomber. That was until one night in 1944 when his plane was critically damaged by German guns, and he and his navigator were forced to bale out.

Gantry parachuted straight into enemy hands, and spent a year in a prisoner-of-war camp, before escaping and returning to Britain with the aid of the French Resistance. Gantry never flew again, but towards the end of the war he took a vital role in RAF Bomber Command.

Twenty years later, back in civilian life, Gantry and his wife were having lunch in a restaurant in their home town, when a man approached their table. Gantry vaguely recognized him, but couldn't place the face.

'Afternoon, Sir. If I might interrupt you, are you by any chance Group Captain Gantry late of Bomber Command? You flew 50 times over enemy territory before being shot down, if I'm not mistaken.'

'I am indeed,' responded the pilot. 'How the devil did you know that?'

'Well, Sir, you probably don't remember me too well. Airman Arthur Chambers, as was. I packed your parachute the night you got shot down – I assume it worked, Sir?'

Gantry jumped up and shook Chambers warmly by the hand. 'It did indeed – otherwise I wouldn't be here now!'

Gantry was bothered all night, thinking about the man he had met that day. He kept wondering just how many times he might have seen him and not even said, 'Hello, how are you today?' because, of course, he was a pilot and Chambers was just an ordinary, lowly airman.

Gantry thought of the many hours this airman had spent at a table carefully folding the silk of each parachute, each time holding in his hands the fate of someone he didn't even know.

'Who's packing your parachute?'

Each of us has someone who provides what we need to make it through the day.

Sometimes in the rush of each day, we miss what is really important.

We may fail to say hello, congratulate someone on something wonderful that has happened to them, give a compliment, or just do something nice for no reason. We may not think to say thank you to our parents and carers, teachers and support staff.

As you go through this week, this month, this year, recognize all the people who pack your parachute.

PUTTING OTHERS FIRST

Many, many years ago a king ordered that a great race should be held in his kingdom, and all the greatest and best athletes should be invited to compete. The prize was to be a bag of pure gold, which would be presented to the winner.

The king personally started the race before returning in his coach to the winning line, which was at the gates of the palace. There he waited to greet the winner. Halfway through the race, however, the runners discovered a huge pile of stones and rocks blocking the road that led to the king's palace. The runners were able to clamber over the rocks or find a path around them, and despite this setback they eventually made it to the gates of the palace.

At last all the runners had crossed the finishing line – all except one, that is. Nevertheless, the king did not declare the race to be over. Eventually one lone runner came running through the gate. He raised a bleeding and bruised hand and said, 'Your Majesty, I am very sorry that I am so late. But you see, I found a pile of rocks and stones in the road, and it took me some time, and I injured myself in removing them.' Then he lifted his other hand, in which was a bag. He said, 'But, Sire, underneath the pile of rocks I found this bag of gold.'

The king said, 'My son, you have won the race, for the one who runs best is he who makes the way safer for those who follow.'

The last runner was rewarded because he took responsibility for what was wrong.

If a chair falls over in class, do you pick it up, or walk round it? If an accident occurs or you do wrong, do you own up or say , 'It's not my fault'? Do you consider the needs of others before your own?

Perhaps helping others is its own reward.

LEARNING FROM EXPERIENCE

Michael was 21 and had been working for a major internet company for just a year when he was unexpectedly promoted to the post of area manager. He'd never imagined that he would rise so far so fast, much less at such a young age. So he went to see Mr Magister, the Managing Director.

'I was wondering if you could give me some advice,' said Michael sheepishly.

Mr Magister didn't even look up from his work and responded with just two words: 'Right decisions!'

The young area manager had hoped for a bit more than this, so he said, 'Thank you, Sir, that's really very useful, and I'm grateful to you, but could you be a bit more precise? *How* do I ensure that I make right decisions?'

The old man responded, 'Experience.'

Michael said, 'Well, that's just the point of my being here. I don't have the kind of experience I need. How do I *get* it?'

Without a moment's hesitation, Mr Magister replied, '*Wrong* decisions!'

There is only one thing more painful than learning from experience, and that is not learning from experience. We all make mistakes from time to time, but it is important to learn from them!

STAY ALERT

It was 1870. The position of wireless operator had recently become available at the local Steamship Office in Southampton. On the day of the interviews a large group of hopeful candidates filled the little waiting room with such a drone of conversation that they were unaware of the sound of dots and dashes that began coming over the loudspeaker.

About this time another man entered and sat down quietly by himself. Suddenly he jumped to attention, walked into the private office, and then came out smiling.

'Oi,' one of the group called out, 'how did you get in there ahead of us? We were all here first.'

'One of you would certainly have got the job,' he replied, 'if you had listened to the message from the loudspeaker.'

'What message?' they all asked in surprise.

'Why, the Morse code,' the stranger answered. 'It said: "The man I need must always be on the alert. The man who gets this message and comes directly into my private office will be placed on one of my ships as an operator."'

Are you always alert to opportunities or do you allow your attention to wander to unimportant things?

THE SOUND OF SILENCE

Four monks decided to meditate silently without speaking for two weeks.

By nightfall on the first day, the candle began to flicker and then went out.

The first monk said, 'Oh, no! The candle is out.'

The second monk said, 'Aren't we supposed not to talk?'

The third monk said, 'Why must you two break the silence?'

The fourth monk laughed and said, 'Ha! I'm the only one who didn't speak.'

Who is the most foolish in this story? The first monk for breaking the silence? The second and third for following without thinking? Or the fourth for imagining himself so much better than his companions?

Do you find it hard to stick to your promises, especially when your friends are equally unreliable?

THE WISE MAN'S STONE

A wise man who was travelling across the mountains of a sacred land found a precious stone in a stream. The next day he met a fellow traveller who was hungry, and the wise man opened his bag to share his food.

The hungry traveller saw the precious stone and asked the man to give it to him. Much to the hungry man's surprise, he did so without hesitation. The traveller left in high spirits – amazed at his good fortune. He knew the stone was worth enough to give him security for the rest of his life.

However, a few days later, the hungry man came back to return the stone to the wise man. 'I've been thinking,' he said. 'I know how valuable this stone is, but I'm giving it back in the hope that you can give me something even more precious. Give me what you have within you that allowed you to give me this stone.'

The hungry man gave back the stone in the hope of getting something better. What's more important to you than wealth?

USING OUR TALENTS WISELY

At the beginning of the twentieth century, a man was caught by the police for forging a five pound note and attempting to deposit it in the bank. The deception was discovered by the cashier who, as she took the note from him, felt that there was something sticky on her fingers. It was this that led her to tell the police that the five pound note might not be genuine.

The police caught the man as he was standing in his attic in front of his easel, in the very act of counterfeiting another five pound note. Unusually the man counterfeited his five pound notes, not through printing, but by painting them. The man was so talented in the art of painting that he could paint a note that was indistinguishable from the real thing.

He had been committing forgery in this way for some time. The reason he had got caught that day was that he had grown impatient and hadn't waited for the paint to get properly dry.

In that attic, police also found three fantastic paintings that the man had painted. The proof of how talented an artist he was lies in the fact that each of the three paintings was later sold for five hundred pounds, which was a lot of money in those days.

Now we could say, 'Oh, well! The man was lazy. He wanted easy money. This is what he did for a quick buck.' And yet it took him the same amount of time to paint a five pound note as it took him to paint a five hundred pound painting! The man had a talent, he worked hard, but he did not know how to put his talent to good use.

It is important to remember that our talents are only as good as the use we make of them. Impatience and lack of commitment can result in their being wasted.

THE BLACK DOOR – FEAR OF THE UNKNOWN

During a particularly long and unpleasant war, which had raged for many years, a spy found that he had been betrayed. Despite his attempts to escape back to his own country, the spy was captured and sentenced to death by firing squad – as was the custom in that land. As the spy was led out into a draughty courtyard to face his fate, he noticed to his left a wall full of small bullet holes – this was clearly where he would meet his end. However, before he could dwell on this terrible thought, he also noticed to his right a large, beautifully decorated black door. Suddenly his attention was caught by the sight of a man in the uniform of a general coming towards him.

Despite his obvious importance and the many shiny medals gleaming on his chest, the general looked like a kindly old man – quite unsuited to the role of a man of war. The general looked the spy straight in the eye and told him in a soft voice that he had a choice – he could either face the firing squad or pass through the large Black Door. The spy was allowed ten minutes to decide, and was directed to sit down in the centre of the courtyard.

As the moment of execution drew near, the general ordered the spy to be brought before him to receive the doomed man's answer to the question: 'Which shall it be – the firing squad or the Black Door?' This was not an easy question, and the prisoner hesitated, but then made it known that he preferred the firing squad. Ninety seconds later a volley of shots in the courtyard proclaimed that the grim sentence had been carried out.

The general turned to his assistant and said sadly, 'You see how it is with most people. They will always prefer the known way to the unknown.'

'What lies beyond the Black Door?' asked the aide.

'Freedom,' replied the general, 'and I've known only a few men brave enough to take it.'

Do you fear the unknown? Perhaps sometimes you should walk through the 'Black Door' – you never know, it might bring you freedom.

THE TWO LIONS

An elderly sage was educating his young disciples about life.

He told them, 'A battle is going on within me. It is a dreadful battle and it is between two great lions. One lion is wicked: he is fear, rage, jealousy, sadness, greed, pride, self-pity, shame, hatred, weakness, lies, rivalry and superiority. The other lion is good: he is happiness, harmony, love, trust, sharing, peace, modesty, gentleness, compassion, friendship, understanding, charity, truth, kindness and loyalty. This same battle is going on inside you and inside every other person as well.'

The disciples considered these words for a while. Then one disciple asked his teacher, 'Which lion will win?'

The old sage replied thoughtfully, 'The one you feed the most.'

Which of the two lions within you do you make the stronger?

ENCOURAGEMENT

Dante Gabriel Rossetti, the famous nineteenth-century poet and artist, was once approached by an elderly man. The old fellow had some sketches and drawings that he wanted Rossetti to look at and tell him if they were any good, or at least indicated potential talent. Rossetti looked them over carefully. After looking at the first few, he knew that they were worthless. They showed not the least sign of artistic talent. But Rossetti was a kind man, and he told the elderly man as gently as possible that the pictures were without much value and showed little talent. He was sorry, but he could not lie to the man.

The visitor was disappointed, but seemed to expect Rossetti's judgement. He then apologized for taking up Rossetti's time, but asked him if he would just look at a few more drawings, which had been painted by a young art student. Rossetti looked over the second batch of sketches and immediately became enthusiastic.

'These,' he said, 'oh, these are good. This young student has great talent. He should be given every help and encouragement in his career as an artist. He has a great future if he will work hard and stick to it.' Rossetti could see that the old fellow was deeply moved. 'Who is this fine young artist?' he asked. 'Your son?'

'No,' said the old man sadly. 'It is me – 40 years ago. If only I had heard your praise then! For you see, I got discouraged and gave up – too soon.'

From Brian Cavanaugh's The Sower's Seeds

A word of praise and encouragement can often be all it takes to transform a person's life. Resolve today to say something positive when asked for your advice.

ANYBODY COULD HAVE DONE IT

Once upon a time, there were four people.

Their names were Everybody, Somebody, Nobody and Anybody.

Whenever there was an important job to be done, Everybody was sure that Somebody would do it.

Anybody could have done it, but Nobody did it.

When Nobody did it, Everybody got angry because it was Everybody's job.

Everybody thought that Somebody would do it, but Nobody realized that Everybody wouldn't do it.

So in the end Everybody blamed Somebody when Nobody did what Anybody could have done in the first place.

Which one are you?